THE HISTORY OF PHILOSOPHY

THE · HISTORY · OF
PHILOSOPHY

A READER'S GUIDE

INCLUDING A LIST OF
100 GREAT PHILOSOPHICAL WORKS
FROM THE PRE-SOCRATICS TO
THE MID-TWENTIETH CENTURY

DONALD PHILLIP VERENE

NORTHWESTERN UNIVERSITY PRESS
EVANSTON, ILLINOIS

Northwestern University Press
www.nupress.northwestern.edu

Printed in the United States of America

10 9 8 7 6 5 4 3 2 1

Library of Congress Cataloging-in-Publication Data

Verene, Donald Phillip, 1937–
        The history of philosophy : a reader's guide : including a
list of 100 great philosophical works from the pre-socratics to
the mid-twentieth century / Donald Phillip Verene
        p. cm.
        Includes bibliographical references and index.
        ISBN-13: 978-0-8101-5197-0 (pbk. : alk. paper)
        ISBN-10: 0-8101-5197-9 (pbk. : alk. paper)
        1. Philosophy—History. I. Title.
        B72.V465 2008
        190—dc22
                                                2007049750

∞ The paper used in this publication meets the minimum requirements of the
American National Standard for Information Sciences—Permanence of Paper
for Printed Library Materials, ANSI Z39.48-1992.

In memory of

Albert William Levi

(1911–1988)

Doctrines must take their beginning from that of
the matters of which they treat.
　　　—Giambattista Vico, *The New Science,* 1.2.106

He who considers things in their first growth
and origin, whether a state or anything else, will
obtain the clearest view of them.
　　　　　　—Aristotle, *Politics,* 1.2

CONTENTS

Preface   xi

PART 1: PHILOSOPHICAL PROPAEDEUTICS

1   Introduction: On the Historical
Study of Philosophy   5

2   100 Great Philosophical Works   17

3   The History of Philosophy in Outline   23

PART 2: PHILOSOPHICAL PERSPECTIVES

4   On Reading Philosophical Books   79

5   The Origin of Philosophy and the
Theater of the World   105

6   Two Views of History and the
History of Philosophy   127

PART 3: PHILOSOPHICAL PRACTICS

7   Philosophical Writing   147

8   Philosophical Literacy   157

Notes   175

Index   183

It was understood for generations that to be an educated person was to be adept in the art of reading, and that reading at its best meant reading the classics, ancient and modern, of the Western canon. A liberal education in historical, literary, and philosophical comprehension became a popular ideal in the first half of the twentieth century and persisted into the 1960s. This general interest was evidenced by Ezra Pound's *How to Read* (1931); by a nationally sold paperback prepared by the Committee on College Reading of the College English Association containing a list of "100 Significant Books," *Good Reading*, which, originally published in 1935, went through more than fifteen reprintings in the 1940s and 1950s; and by Mortimer Adler's Chicago-based efforts to promote a curriculum of the "Great Books" and to conduct reading and discussion groups for the general public.

During the last half of the twentieth century the desire for such an education waned and finally fell under the weight of the criticism that the Western canon was biased in every sense—as to gender, race, ethnicity, and class. The canon was declared not just biased but unforgivable and unredeemable. In early 1988 students held a rally at Stanford University with Jesse Jackson, where they chanted, "Hey hey, ho ho, Western culture's got to go!" Countering this attitude is Bernard Knox's *The Oldest Dead European White Males and Other Reflections on the Classics* and Harold Bloom's elegy, *The Western Canon: The Books and Schools of the Ages*. Bloom says, with great regret, that he does not expect to see the canon resurrected, although he does his best in *The Western Canon*, with a lively version based on the ages of Giambattista Vico's cyclic view of history, coupled with James Joyce's expansion of it.

The study of the history of philosophy has always been canonically conceived. This conception can be found in the doxographical histories of philosophy of the ancients as well as in Jakob Brucker's five-volume *Critical History of Philosophy* (1742–67) and Hegel's *Lectures on the History of Philosophy*. But the history of philosophy has had much the same fate as the general Western canon. In the second half of the twentieth century, Anglo-American analytic philosophy and continental philosophy each in its own way took a critical stand on the history of philosophy. Logical positivism and ordinary-language analysis saw philosophy in ahistorical terms, as irrelevant to their aims of clarifying the claims of science and explicating the insights of ordinary language. Philosophy had become so insular and remote from general culture and human concerns that *Time* magazine (January 7, 1966) published an essay with the title "What (If Anything) to Expect from Today's Philosophers." The conclusion was: very little.

The most aggressive view of the unimportance of the history of philosophy for philosophy was expressed in the early phases of American analytic circles by the claim that the study of the history of philosophy was "like reading names and inscriptions on tombstones." In this view, the history of philosophy is not a treasure-house of ideas from which to think but is merely a repository of errors that can at most be the subject of idle curiosity, and what is needed in philosophy is to be free of the past. A view circulated among American adherents to ordinary-language philosophy in its heyday in the 1950s and 1960s declared that all that was needed to do philosophy was "the *Oxford English Dictionary* and a pencil." These were extreme but commonly expressed views that are not usually heard today, but they captured the attitude that the history of philosophy is not a basis for proper philosophical education. Ironically, both of these movements have themselves become part of the history of philosophy.

In continental philosophy, although populated by philosophers with European literary educations, there arose a distrust of any inclusive or synthetic historical narratives. Based on the works of Marx, Freud, and Nietzsche—whom Paul Ricoeur identified as the "masters of suspicion"—there arose the general doctrine of the "hermeneutics of suspicion." According to this doctrine, what philosophers traditionally thought to be the pursuit of truth that took them beyond the limits of their own times was, in reality, the reflection of economic class, psychosexual dominance, and cultural and religious bias. The basis of traditional philosophies, in this view, could be uncovered through clever exposition and interrogation of their premises. Jacques Derrida's "White Mythology" is a complicated example of the unveiling, the "deconstruction," of traditional views of Western philosophy. To study the history of philosophy from the standpoint of the "hermeneutics of suspicion" is to reveal the deceptions embedded in the great philosophical systems and narratives of the past.

The extreme views of the history of philosophy expressed at mid-twentieth century and beyond have become modified. As negative views they provided little content for sustained discussion. The adherents of both analytic and continental philosophy have taken up arguments, problems, and themes found in the works of historical figures. The works of Derrida, Michel Foucault, and the French generally abound with historical material. But with this activity there has not come a revival or endorsement of the canonical sense of the history of philosophy.

Despite the aversion to the Western canon within the world of letters generally and the aversion to the study of the history of philosophy in particular, interest in the canon has prevailed. There are those who will not give it up and who still desire the education that the great works can provide. I am one of those who would wish to sail between the Scylla of analysis and the Charybdis of suspicion, with the desire to return to the Ithaca of the canon. To understand what I intend by the list of 100 great philosophical works in chapter 2, I refer the reader to my comments on the nature of a canon in the introductory chapter. The list of 100 great philosophical works is not intended as a perfect or a hard-and-fast list, and the overview or outline of the history of philosophy that follows the list, in chapter 3, is intended as an indication of the periods, figures, and major and minor works to be kept in mind in the study of the history of philosophy. I have presented this in schematic form. It does not purport to be a history of philosophy. For that one must go to the histories of philosophy listed at the end of the outline.

The outline is an interpretation of the history of philosophy. Because the canon has disappeared so much from our consciousness, the outline provides an overview, a reminder of what is there in the history of philosophy. The reader may wish first to look at the outline, then move on to the essays of part 2, and from them to come back to the outline as a guide to think through and absorb its order. The method of this book is not that of a linear argument. It is set up dialectically, with interplay between the two rhetorical forms of presentation, *narratio* and *ratio,* the narration (the essays) versus the list and outline. It may thus serve the reader as a touchstone and a guide to return to at various times—to enter the reading of works in the history of philosophy or to discover those works and movements of which perhaps the reader was not well aware.

The list of 100 great works and those works in the outline as well as the commentaries on them which are interspersed throughout the outline are drawn from the resources of my personal library. The commentaries are selected from ones I have used. Very likely there are glaring omissions. I have generally not included commentaries on individual thinkers, only works on periods or movements. It has not been my intention to write a textbook, taking a neutral position on the subject. This book is directed toward anyone who may have an interest in the history of philosophy and who may find what it presents useful.

This personal approach is evident in the three essays that follow in part 2. The first offers a view of philosophical reading and the philosophical use of language; the second a view of the origin of philosophy and the philosopher developed through the speculative use of the history of philosophy, moving from ancient to Renaissance to modern; and the third an exposition of how the philosophy of history affects the conception of the history of philosophy, using Vico and Hegel as holders of two views. These essays present rhetorical, humanist, and historical perspectives on the study and nature of philosophy and the history of philosophy. They are intended as suggestive rather than definitive accounts, with which the reader should feel free to disagree. As with the particular canon that each reader must develop from the larger, more general canon of the history of philosophy, each reader must come to some conclusions about the meaning of this history, about what aspects of it make it agile and alive.

Because some may wish not only to read the history of philosophy but also to write about it, I have included some practical advice on this topic in part 3, as well as a chapter on philosophical literacy containing 700 terms, names, and works that should be known or become known to those who study the history of philosophy and the field of philosophy generally. These are all taken from standard encyclopedias and reference works in philosophy. To my knowledge no one has as yet advanced such a literacy list in philosophy. It may interest the reader as a simple gauge of what should be philosophical common knowledge.

I thank my colleagues who have read versions of this work: Thora Bayer, Ann Hartle, George Benjamin Kleindorfer, Donald Livingston, David Lovekin, Fred Marcus, Nancy Marcus, John McCumber, Michael Sullivan, William Willeford, and Cynthia Willett. I am grateful to more than a generation of students, both graduate and undergraduate, who have influenced my thinking on the study of the history of philosophy. I extend particular thanks to Henry L. Carrigan Jr. of Northwestern University Press for his great kindness and attention during the editorial process of this book. Finally, I thank Molly Black Verene, whose technical work and substantive advice on the manuscript have been indispensable.

THE HISTORY OF PHILOSOPHY

PART 1

Philosophical Propaedeutics

INTRODUCTION: ON THE
HISTORICAL STUDY OF PHILOSOPHY

Philosophical Education

The aim of this book is to offer a guide to what Hegel calls "the long process of education towards genuine philosophy."[1] The mark of philosophical culture is the ability of its practitioner to carry on a conversation with its past. The reason to carry on this conversation with the past is to become a philosopher. Education is the past revived by memory and brought to bear on the present. This revivification requires a friendship with those who have written the great philosophical works. Only through a friendship with the past is new philosophy born. The modern agora, or marketplace of ideas, is history. In the agora of history all known philosophies are able to present themselves and speak to the contemporary thinker. The great conversation of the liberal arts, of which philosophy is properly a part, is a conversation with the past, not as something fixed and dead, but as alive and agile. The history of philosophy is a whole, not the whole of a single truth, but a whole in the sense of a temporal totality, a totality of what is, was, and will be. Without memory there is no culture, and without its own memory there is no philosophy. As the human self requires memory to make and maintain its identity, so philosophy requires its memory for its identity. Philosophy without memory has no inner form; it is a vacuous actuality, a logical exercise, a form of debate.

Philosophy is as hindered by the avoidance of argument and by confinement to prescribed study as it is by the purely argumentative approach. Misology, or the hatred of argument, as Socrates says in the *Phaedo* (89d), is a philosophical vice. But argument requires the rhetorical power of language to bring forth, from human experience and from the meanings of words, the starting points of rational thought that argument itself cannot provide. Logic never supplies its own starting points. The production of these beginnings and the process of their logical development stand to each other as counterparts—as strophe to antistrophe. Internal to philosophical conversation and thought is the movement between these two poles. The end of philosophical education, as with human education generally, is style. The great works of philosophy are the source, not only of what may be said but of how it may be said, the possibilities of language to express the true, the good, and the beautiful, although the wisdom that the philosopher loves is never fully captured in words. In philosophy as elsewhere, the new is always born from the old.

There are two ways to comprehend the history of philosophy. It can be regarded purely historically or it can be regarded philosophically. The history of philosophy is first and foremost history. As history the history of philosophy can be understood as intellectual history, as a part of the history of ideas of Western thought. To treat the history of philosophy as a part of intellectual history is to explicate the sources and influences of the figures, movements, and periods it contains and to connect them with the forms of society and culture in which they occur. Intellectual historians, in interpreting a particular philosopher, often proceed as if all that can be said is said when the precedents and sources of the philosopher's thought and works have been elicited, when these have been placed in their own time and their influences shown. This is rightly the most that can be accomplished from the standpoint and methods of the intellectual historian, and it is indispensable for the student of the history of philosophy. The full study of a given philosopher requires an understanding of what is known of the philosopher's life, times, and ideas, and the place of these ideas in the historical development of philosophy.

Beyond the historical comprehension of the history of philosophy is its comprehension as philosophy. The philosopher approaches the history of philosophy where the historian leaves off. The philosopher is concerned with the truth of what a given figure in the history of philosophy has said once the philological and historical meanings of what he said have been established. This philosophical concern for truth takes two forms: critical and speculative. The critical understanding of philosophical ideas is essentially reflective. Critical scholarship focuses on evaluating the coherence, comprehension, and evidence for the arguments, claims, and doctrines held by any given historical figure or philosophical position. Critical thinking by its nature aims at evaluating the truth or falsity of what it examines. Any figure or part of the history of philosophy can be the subject of this critical, reflective examination and interpretation. The critical approach as such produces no new ideas. It aids the student of philosophy to settle on what is said by historical figures and movements and to access them logically, evidentially, and hermeneutically.

The critical approach takes a stand outside what any philosopher in the history of philosophy says; it takes what is said as an object of investigation, a subject matter. In contrast to this, the speculative approach seeks out the inner form of what a historical figure says and how that philosopher's thought is formed. To consider the history of philosophy speculatively is to see it as a basis for philosophizing, for continuing the processes of insight and reasoning exemplified by the great figures in the history of philosophy. The critical approach reasons about some part of the contents of the history of philosophy. The speculative approach selects some aspects of the contents and uses the interpretations it develops as the ground for further philosophizing. What the speculative student hopes to learn from the history of philosophy and its figures is how to philosophize, how to attain the inside of philosophy by penetrating the thoughts of its greatest practitioners. The critical approach can manifest elements of the speculative, but the principles of its reflective study cause it to stop short of the speculative. The speculative presupposes and employs the results of the critical, but its ultimate intent is not simply the evaluation of ideas. The great philosophers of the canon all manifest this speculative standpoint. They take from their predecessors what is needed to communicate and continue their philosophical vision. The critical approach walks around its object from the outside. The speculative approach goes to the object's inside, and penetrates its inner being.

It is rightly said in the study of philosophy that the most inaccurate interpretative claims about the views of great philosophers are to be found in the works of other great philosophers. Great philosophers take what they need from others. The speculative approach, when practiced on a less grand scale, must hold to a more modest standard. But the speculative approach makes ideas come alive. It pursues the fundamental truths preserved in the history of philosophy, takes instruction from them, and resurrects them for the furtherance of the love of wisdom. In this way the history of philosophy becomes more than a subject for scholarship. "Truth is the daughter of time" in the sense that the past makes the present what it is. To study the history of philosophy speculatively is to philosophize in terms of it and in so doing to give new shape to the spirit of philosophy.

To philosophize in the thin air of the present, uninvolved with the past, is to argue with one's contemporaries, to cut oneself off from the forms of imagination and memory that can be found only in the past. The history of philosophy is part of the great conversation of the republic of letters of the liberal arts, the arts which humanize. To restrict philosophy largely or wholly to the life of the present is to make it less than human, to cut philosophy off from itself, to make it a smaller thing. As with a human self, whose own story enters into each significant moment of its activity, so with philosophy—its story is the guide to its present speech. Each of the great philosophers is a complete university. Unless one decides to read the great philosophers simply for pleasure, which in itself is a legitimate and noble goal, the reason for reading them is to become a philosopher. Thinking of his own pursuit of natural philosophy through the direct observation of nature, Galileo expressed in memorable fashion what is required to become a philosopher in any sense of the term.

The difference between philosophizing and studying philosophy is that which exists between drawing from nature and copying pictures. In order to become accustomed to handling the pen or crayon in good style, it is right to begin by redrawing good pictures created by excellent artists. Likewise in order to stimulate the mind and guide it toward good philosophy, it is useful to observe the things that have already been investigated by others in their philosophizing; especially those which are true and certain, these being chiefly mathematical.

But men who go on forever copying pictures and never get around to drawing from nature can never become perfect artists, or even good judges of painting. For they remain unpracticed in separating the good from the bad, or the accurately from the poorly drawn, by means of recognizing in nature itself (as a result of countless experiences) the true effects of foreshortening, of backgrounds, of lights and shadows, of reflections, and of the infinite variations in differing viewpoints.

In the same way a man will never become a philosopher by worrying forever about the writings of other men, without ever raising his own eyes to nature's works in the attempt to recognize there the truths already known and to investigate some of the infinite number that remain to be discovered. This, I say, will never make a man a philosopher, but only a student of other philosophers and an expert in their works.[2]

Tetralogy: Plato and Aristotle, Kant and Hegel

The 100 great philosophical works that precede the outline of the history of philosophy in chapter 3 are the skeleton of the canon. These 100 works can be comprehended only in terms of their connections with the further works noted in the outline, which provide a corpus for the skeleton of the list. To give the canon shape as a history and to aid in its study, some commentaries are listed that illuminate the various periods in this history. The heart of the corpus is the tetralogy of Plato and Aristotle, Kant and Hegel. The first pair, Plato and Aristotle, divide ancient philosophy between them. Medieval through Renaissance philosophy is incomprehensible without a command of the ideas of Platonic and Aristotelian thought. The second two, Kant and Hegel, are the pillars of modern philosophy. The systems of modern rationalism and empiricism cannot be understood apart from their summation in Kantian critique. Kant is needed to understand Leibniz and Locke. The methods of dialectical materialism and pragmatism cannot be comprehended apart from the Hegelian conception of experience. Hegel is needed to understand Marx and Dewey and also to understand Kant. The study of the whole history of philosophy emanates from the mastery of the major works of the two great ancients and the two great moderns.

Aristotle both continues and opposes Plato's doctrine of the forms with his doctrine of the individual existent, and he continues and transforms the Platonic doctrine of virtue and the state into an ethics and politics. Goethe says that "Plato relates himself to the world as a blessed spirit, whom it pleases sometimes to stay for a while in the world." But "Aristotle, on the contrary, stands to the world as a man, an architect. He is only here once and must here make and create."[3] Both of these souls live in almost all our great thinkers. This double soul of philosophy is preserved in the Middle Ages and resurrected in the Renaissance. Through the rich visions of the Renaissance, philosophy is brought forward for the modern world. The sense of critical judgment of the

Enlightenment guides Kant. The need for a sense of the speculative judgment guides Hegel.

Hegel both continues and opposes Kant's idealism in moving from transcendental critique to the dialectic of the speculative sentence and in moving from the categorical imperative as the logic of moral judgment to the forms of ethical and social life comprehended as a development of spirit. In the introduction to the *Critique of Pure Reason*, thinking of Plato's *Phaedrus*, Kant says: "The light dove, cleaving the air in her free flight, and feeling its resistance, might imagine that its flight would be still easier in empty space. It was thus that Plato left the world of the senses, as setting too narrow limits to the understanding, and ventured out beyond it on the wings of the ideas, in the empty space of the pure understanding."[4] Through his transcendental method of philosophical reflection, Kant will stand firmly on the earth within experience but allow the thing-in-itself to be outside our experience.

Hegel begins the *Phenomenology of Spirit* with the thing-in-itself as the object of sense-certainty, and through the dialectical exposition of illusion after illusion he penetrates to the inner form of the "in-itself and the for-itself" until the true as the whole comes into consciousness as the absolute. Hegel calls this dialectical exposition "the science of the experience of consciousness." This science presupposes the entire study of the history of philosophy, yet, Hegel claims, many would think philosophy can be done directly from the use of our powers of ratiocination. Hegel says: "When it comes to philosophy, there seems to be a currently prevailing prejudice to the effect that, although not everyone who has eyes and fingers, and is given leather and last, is at once in a position to make shoes, everyone nevertheless immediately understands how to philosophize, and how to evaluate philosophy, since he possesses the criterion for doing so in his natural reason—as if he did not likewise possess the measure for a shoe in his own foot."[5] Hegel's metaphor plays on the proverb "ne sutor ultra crepidam" (the shoemaker should stick to his last), employed when a shoemaker attempts to be an art critic in Pliny's *Natural History* (35.85).

The combination of Kant and Hegel opens the door to the critical and the historical. Without them we cannot understand the modern world. They are its threshold. The ideas captured in the philosophies of Plato and Aristotle, Kant and Hegel, circulate like the blood throughout the whole corpus of philosophy.

The Idea of a Canon

The Western canon presumes that philosophy, which takes its name from the Greeks, also takes itself from them. All great histories of philosophy, such as those that appear among the works of general interest at the end of the outline in chapter 3, presuppose that philosophy as the rational inquiry into the fundamental nature of all things human and divine is a Western invention, tied to the development of Western culture. I say this while fully acknowledging the indispensable influence of the scholarship and thought of the Middle East during the eleventh and twelfth centuries.

Although philosophy is an invention of the Greeks, the proper study of philosophy cannot exclude the study of sacred texts and systems of wisdom. Among these are the Babylonian *Enuma Elish* and *Epic of Gilgamesh,* the Egyptian Book of the Dead, the Hebrew Bible, the New Testament, the Cabala, the Zohar, *Corpus Hermeticum,* and *Asclepius,* the Vedas, Upanishads, Bhagavad Gītā, The Life of the Buddha, Lotus Sūtra, Lankâvatâra Sūtra, the Analects, the Qur'ān (Koran), Sufi writings, the I Ching, Tibetan Book of the Dead, Tao Te Ching, Zen stories, and creation myths such as those collected in Barbara Sproul's *Primal Myths.*[6] The reading of such texts provides a partial education in various comprehensions of the real that are not arrived at through a dedication to rational inquiry. For the past three decades I have regularly taught a course in Asian philosophy, emphasizing texts in the Buddhist and Taoist traditions and some basic study of the I Ching. No study of Western philosophy can avoid attention to what lies outside its dedication to critical and speculative reason. Within the great works of philosophy in the West there are many passages that provide points of transition to the ideas of the East. No canon is perfect or final. It is the product of a single mind's eye or of several minds of common vision. A canon is both indispensable and open to criticism. It is indispensable because no one can think without it. Any study of philosophy tacitly or explicitly regards some texts as more fundamental to that study than others. To deny the traditional Western canon is simply to affirm another. To attempt indeterminate study without some sense of a canon is a kind of ignorance. Knowledge requires a standard, and some works will meet this standard more than others. Personal preference is not a standard, nor is convention, for the same reason that they are not knowledge. The critic of the canon is caught like a fly in a bottle. The critic of any canon must revise it or reform it. If not, the critic remains just a critic, unable to accept the task of taking on the formative powers of thought.

There are in principle as many canons of the history of philosophy as there are those who study it. But were another to write out a list of 100 great philosophical works covering the same periods as those in my outline, I expect the list would differ, likely in interesting ways, but not differ greatly, unless the aim was to be deliberately idiosyncratic. A canon, once absorbed, lets one see beyond it to other figures of interest that are not explicitly listed there. Not all figures that are of importance in the history of philosophy and that are discussed in various historical studies need appear in a canon. A canon is predicated on the fact that such figures are there, though unlisted. A canon is not a device to exclude their importance; it is instead a means to come to them. As one studies the canon in chapter 2 and the outline which follows it in chapter 3, one is always led beyond them into the details of the history of philosophy and into its most minor figures. Attention to major figures leads one to minor, often nearly unknown figures.

Contemporary Philosophy

The canon provided in chapter 2 does not go past the mid-twentieth century. Any canon needs historical distance to have a useful sense of fixity. The passage of time and the formation of tradition are needed to produce a genuine canon. Time and tradition include by excluding. How, then, is the study of philosophical works that are contemporary with the generation studying them to proceed? It is a mistake to pretend that there is a canon of contemporary philosophical texts. The present must be read in terms of the past. It cannot be read intelligently in terms of the present. When the present is read from the past, there is an opportunity to see what is new and significant. Any canon of works that appears in one's lifetime is inherently unsatisfying. It is unsatisfying because no perspective is readily forthcoming to focus the mind's eye. The best advice for those studying works of the present can only be to read widely and see what is there.

Those who, for example, would wish to become expert in the thought of Gadamer, Habermas, Levinas, Foucault, or Derrida cannot limit themselves to the study of their works and discussions of them. To understand these thinkers one must also study what they themselves studied, namely, the great works of the history of philosophy. A similar claim can be made of later twentieth-century figures in the development of Anglo-American analytic philosophy. The ideas of Strawson, Goodman, Quine, Sellars, and Rawls did not spring directly from the head of a logical Zeus; they have behind them the earlier traditions of realism, common sense philosophy, and conceptions of science and ethical theory that originated as reactions to nineteenth-century idealism, and such idealism originated in response to what went before it. Although not historical in form, philosophical analysis develops its doctrines in history, and to understand these doctrines, their history, as it is absorbed into the history of philosophy, must be studied.

Although there is no true sense of canon to apply to works of one's own time, the following are some philosophically significant works that are good reading in contemporary philosophy. What works will emerge as crucial to the development of the philosophic spirit in the latter half of the twentieth century and on into the twenty-first century can be ascertained only in retrospect. Some of the works that attract so much attention today will likely fade, in the way that, for example, many works of logical positivism, new and critical realism, and existentialism from the twentieth century have faded. The following book-length works are arranged alphabetically by author and are only the smallest suggestion of contemporary philosophical good reading. I offer this list as a place to start. Since many of the original positions and arguments in Anglo-American analytic philosophy exist as journal articles, the reader may wish to pursue them through the bibliographies available in the works listed under "Commentaries: Twentieth Century" near the end of the outline in chapter 3.

Derrida, Jacques, *Of Grammatology*

Eco, Umberto, *A Theory of Semiotics*

Foucault, Michel, *The Order of Things*

Gadamer, Hans-Georg, *Truth and Method*

Goodman, Nelson, *Ways of Worldmaking*

Habermas, Jürgen, *Knowledge and Human Interests*

Langer, Susanne, *Feeling and Form*

Levinas, Emmanuel, *Totality and Infinity*

Lyotard, Jean-François, *The Postmodern Condition*

MacIntyre, Alasdair, *After Virtue*

Quine, W. V. O., *Word and Object*

Rawls, John, *A Theory of Justice*

Sellars, Wilfred, *Science, Perception and Reality*

Strawson, P. F., *Individuals*

The student of contemporary philosophy who does not read the present in relation to the canon of the past lacks education. Those who work from a canon to comprehend the present are on the right path. But the study of the history of philosophy is not itself philosophy. Philosophy is always more than its history. To philosophize is to think beyond historical conditions. An education in the history of philosophy does not commit one to historicism; philosophy is not confined to what is produced in a given age. As Ernst Cassirer says, "'Truth' is not bound to productive activity and it is not to be measured by its criteria."[7] Truth is always both within and beyond the temporal. What one takes the history of philosophy to be is determined by what one takes philosophy itself to be.

The titles of works in the outline of the history of philosophy in chapter 3 appear almost exclusively in English, reflecting the availability of most works in English translation. Regarding those of the 100 great philosophical works that were not originally written in English, all exist in English translation and often in multiple translations. This approach is not intended to imply that the study of philosophy is to be confined to English texts. The proper study of Western philosophy requires at the least some command of seven languages. One needs ability in English, French, German, Italian, Spanish, Latin, and ancient Greek. Few are likely to know all these languages equally. Specialist study might require ability in other languages, such as Russian or Arabic. At a minimum, fluency in two or three of these modern languages is needed, and a minimum terminological ability and some reading ability should be cultivated in Latin and Greek. If one does not know Greek, F. E. Peters's *Greek Philosophical Terms* is especially useful.[8]

100 GREAT PHILOSOPHICAL WORKS

**FROM THE PRE-SOCRATICS TO THE MID-TWENTIETH CENTURY,
ARRANGED CHRONOLOGICALLY BY AUTHOR'S DATE OF BIRTH**

1. Pre-Socratics, Fragments

2. Plato, *Dialogues*

3. Aristotle, *Works*

4. Cicero, *On Duties*

5. Lucretius, *The Way Things Are*

6. Plutarch, *Moralia* (selections)

7. Lucian, *Philosophers for Sale*

8. Longinus, *On the Sublime*

9. Marcus Aurelius, *Meditations*

10. Plotinus, *Enneads*

11. Sextus Empiricus, *Outlines of Pyrrhonism*

12. Saint Augustine, *Confessions*

13. Boethius, *Consolation of Philosophy*

14. Saint Anselm, *Proslogion*

15. Averroës, *The Incoherence of the Incoherence*

16. Maimonides, *The Guide of the Perplexed*

17. Saint Thomas Aquinas, *Summa Theologiae* (selections)

18. Duns Scotus, *Philosophical Writings*

19. William of Ockham, *Philosophical Writings*

20. Petrarch, *On His Own Ignorance and That of Many Others*

21. Ibn Khaldūn, *The Muqaddima: An Introduction to History*

22. Nicholas of Cusa, *Of Learned Ignorance*

23. Ficino, *Platonic Theology*

24. Pico della Mirandola, "Oration on the Dignity of Man"

25. Erasmus, *The Praise of Folly*

26. Machiavelli, *The Prince*

27. More, *Utopia*

28. Vives, "A Fable About Man"

29. Montaigne, *Essays*

30. Bruno, *The Expulsion of the Triumphant Beast*

31. Suárez, *Metaphysical Disputations* (selections)

32. Bacon, *New Organon*

33. Galileo, *The Assayer*

34. Campanella, *The City of the Sun*

35. Boehme, *Six Theosophic Points*

36. Gracián, *The Art of Worldly Wisdom*

37. Grotius, *The Law of War and Peace*

38. Hobbes, *Leviathan*

39. Descartes, *Discourse on Method*

40. Pascal, *Pensées*

41. Spinoza, *Ethics*

42. Locke, *An Essay Concerning Human Understanding*

43. Malebranche, *The Search After Truth*

44. Leibniz, *Monadology*

45. Bayle, *The Historical and Critical Dictionary* (selections)

46. Vico, *The New Science*

47. Mandeville, *The Fable of the Bees*

48. Shaftesbury, *Characteristics of Men, Manners, Opinions, Times*

49. Wolff, *Preliminary Discourse on Philosophy in General*

50. Berkeley, *A Treatise Concerning the Principles of Human Knowledge*

51. Montesquieu, *Spirit of the Laws*

52. Voltaire, *Candide*

53. Johnson, *The History of Rasselas*

54. La Mettrie, *Man a Machine*

55. Reid, *Inquiry into the Human Mind, or The Principles of Common Sense*

56. Hume, *A Treatise of Human Nature*

57. Rousseau, *First and Second Discourses*

58. Condorcet, *A Historical Tableau of the Progress of the Human Mind*

59. Condillac, *Treatise on the Sensations*

60. d'Alembert, *Preliminary Discourse to the Encyclopedia*

61. Smith, *The Wealth of Nations*

62. Burke, *Reflections on the Revolution in France*

63. Kant, *Critique of Pure Reason*

64. Herder, *Outlines of a Philosophy of the History of Man*

65. Bentham, *An Introduction to the Principles of Morals and Legislation*

66. Schiller, *On the Aesthetic Education of Man in a Series of Letters*

67. Fichte, *Science of Knowledge (Wissenschaftslehre)*

68. Schleiermacher, *On Religion: Speeches to Its Cultured Despisers*

69. Hegel, *Phenomenology of Spirit*

70. Schelling, *System of Transcendental Idealism*

71. Schopenhauer, *The World as Will and Representation*

72. Comte, *The Positive Philosophy* (selections)

73. Feuerbach, *The Essence of Christianity*

74. Mill, *On Liberty*

75. Kierkegaard, *Philosophical Fragments*

76. Marx, *The Economic and Philosophical Manuscripts*

77. Peirce, *Selected Papers*

78. James, *Principles of Psychology*

79. Nietzsche, *On the Genealogy of Morality*

80. Dilthey, *The Formation of the Historical World in the Human Sciences*

81. Bradley, *Appearance and Reality*

82. Berdyaev, *The Destiny of Man*

83. Frege, "On Sense and Reference"

84. Bergson, *Creative Evolution*

85. Dewey, *Experience and Nature*

86. Husserl, *Ideas*

87. Whitehead, *Process and Reality*

88. Santayana, *The Life of Reason*

89. Croce, *Aesthetic as Science of Expression and General Linguistic*

90. Russell, *An Inquiry into Meaning and Truth*

91. Moore, *Principia Ethica*

92. Cassirer, *An Essay on Man*

93. Ortega y Gasset, *The Revolt of the Masses*

94. Collingwood, *An Essay on Philosophical Method*

95. Heidegger, *Being and Time*

96. Wittgenstein, *Tractatus Logico-Philosophicus*

97. Carnap, *Logical Syntax of Language*

98. Ryle, *The Concept of Mind*

99. Sartre, *Being and Nothingness*

100. Austin, *How to Do Things with Words*

THE HISTORY OF
PHILOSOPHY IN OUTLINE

This outline is intended as an overview. The study of it may assist
the reader in placing certain works in certain periods. Should the
reader already be interested in certain periods or movements, the
reader can gain a view of their scope from the outline. Of the
Renaissance, for example, which is the most neglected period
in philosophical education, the reader may quickly gain a view
of its dimensions and figures and find a useful guide in this part
of the outline. The same is true of the Hellenistic period, the
various medieval schools, the range of Enlightenment figures, and
the lesser-known movements of the twentieth century. The brief
schema of the outline below is followed by the outline proper.

Ancient Philosophy

> The Pre-Socratics (600–400 B.C.E.)
>
> Socratic Philosophy
>
> Fourth-Century Hellenic Philosophy
>
> Movements of Hellenistic and Roman Thought

Medieval Philosophy (from the Council of Nicaea [325] to the closing of the School of Athens [529] and the fall of Constantinople [1453])

> Patristic Authors
>
> Early Medieval Philosophers
>
> Islamic Philosophy (800–1400)
>
> Jewish Philosophy (1000–1450)
>
> Thirteenth Century: The "Golden Age" of Scholasticism

Renaissance Philosophy (from 1350 to the early seventeenth century)

> The Italian Philosophers
>
> The Transalpine Thinkers

Modern Philosophy (from Descartes' *Discourse* [1637] to the death of Nietzsche [1900] and the movements of the twentieth century)

> Early Modern Philosophers and Philosophical Systems
>
> Enlightenment and Counter-Enlightenment Thought
>
> German Idealism and Nineteenth-Century Philosophy
>
> Philosophies from the Turn of the Century to the
> Mid-Twentieth Century

ANCIENT PHILOSOPHY

"Philosophy before philosophy." The words belonging to the *philosophia* family did not in fact appear until the fifth century B.C.E., and the term *philosophia* itself was not defined until the fourth century B.C.E., by Plato. Aristotle, however, and with him the entire tradition of the history of philosophy, applied the word "philosophers" to the first Greek thinkers who appeared at the beginning of the sixth century in the colonies of Asia Minor, at the periphery of the Greek zone of influence.

All these thinkers proposed a *rational* explanation of the world—and this was a milestone in the history of thought. To be sure, there had been cosmogonies before them, in the Near East, and elsewhere in Archaic Greece as well. Yet these had been mythical—that is to say, they described the history of the world as a battle among personified entities. They were "geneses" in the biblical sense of the Book of Genesis (or Book of Generations), which was intended to bring a people back to the memory of its ancestors, and to reconnect it with the cosmic forces and generations of the gods. Creation of the world, creation of man, creation of a people: such had been the object of those cosmogonies. Although the first Greek thinkers substituted a rational theory of the world for such mythical narratives, they still preserved the three-part schema which had structured the older cosmogonies. They proposed a theory to explain the origins of the world, of mankind, and of the city.

—Pierre Hadot, *What Is Ancient Philosophy?*

THE PRE-SOCRATICS (600–400 B.C.E.)

On the Origin of Philosophy

F. M. Cornford, *From Religion to Philosophy: A Study in the Origins of Western Speculation.*

———, *Principium Sapientiae: The Origins of Greek Philosophical Thought.*

H. Frankfort and others, *The Intellectual Adventure of Ancient Man: An Essay on Speculative Thought in the Ancient Near East.*

T. H. Gaster, *Thespis: Ritual, Myth and Drama in the Ancient Near East.*

B. Snell, *The Discovery of the Mind: The Greek Origins of European Thought.*

Fragments of the Pre-Socratic Philosophers

H. Diels and W. Kranz, *Die Fragmente der Vorsokratiker,* 6th ed., 3 vols. Standard edition of the Greek texts of the fragments, with German translation.

J. Barnes, ed. and trans., *Early Greek Philosophy.* Anthology.

K. Freeman, *Companion to the Pre-Socratic Philosophers.*

———, *Ancilla to the Pre-Socratic Philosophers: A Complete Translation of the Fragments in Diels, Fragmente der Vorsokratiker.*

G. S. Kirk, J. E. Raven, and M. Schofield, *The Presocratic Philosophers,* 2nd ed. Selection of texts with English translation and commentary.

Principal Figures

The Ionians

The Milesian school: Thales, Anaximander, Anaximenes

Xenophanes of Colophon (emigrated to Sicily and southern Italy)

Heraclitus of Ephesus

Pythagoreanism
Pythagoras of Samos

The Pythagorean school, at Croton, in southern Italy

Philolaus

The Eleatics
The Eleatic school: Parmenides, Zeno, Melissus of Samos (Ionian Greek colony of Elea in southern Italy)

The Pluralists
Empedocles (born in Acragas [Agrigento], Sicily)

Anaxagoras of Clazomenae

Atomists: Leucippus and Democritus (Abderites, school of Abdera)

Diogenes of Apollonia

The Sophists
Protagoras of Abdera

Gorgias of Leontini

Prodicus of Ceos

Thrasymachus of Chalcedon in Bithynia

Hippias of Elis

See *The Older Sophists: A Complete Translation*, ed. R. K. Sprague.

Commentaries: Pre-Socratic Philosophy

P. Curd, *The Legacy of Parmenides.*

K. S. Guthrie and others, comp. and trans., *The Pythagorean Sourcebook and Library*, new ed.

W. K. C. Guthrie, *A History of Greek Philosophy:* vol. 1, *The Earlier Presocratics and the Pythagoreans;* vol. 2, *The Presocratic Tradition from Parmenides to Democritus.*

W. Jaeger, *The Theology of the Early Greek Philosophers.*

C. H. Kahn, *The Art and Thought of Heraclitus.*

———, *Anaximander and the Origins of Greek Cosmology.*

———, *Pythagoras and the Pythagoreans: A Brief History.*

H. D. P. Lee, *Zeno of Elea.* Translation and commentary.

R. D. McKirahan, *Philosophy Before Socrates: An Introduction with Texts and Commentary.*

Socratic Philosophy

Socrates

The Last Days of Socrates: Euthyphro, Apology, Crito, Phaedo, trans. H. Tredennick and H. Tarrant.

Aristophanes, *The Clouds,* trans. W. Arrowsmith.

Xenophon, *Memorabilia.*

See also T. C. Brickhouse and N. D. Smith, *The Trial and Execution of Socrates: Sources and Controversies.*

The Socratic Schools

The Megarians (fourth and early third centuries B.C.E.)

Euclides, founder of the seat at Megara and friend of Socrates; merged Eleatic tradition with Socratic philosophy

Eubulides, Euclides' successor and a contemporary and critic of Aristotle

Stilpo, rival of Theophrastus and a teacher of the Stoic Zeno

Diodorus Cronus, also a teacher of the Stoic Zeno

The Cyrenaics (second half of the fourth and first quarter of the third century B.C.E.)

Aristippus of Cyrene, friend of Socrates, originating figure of the Cyrenaics' hedonistic philosophy

The Cyrenaics include Arete (child of Aristippus), Aristippus (child of Arete), Hegesias, Anniceris, and Theodorus.

The Cynics (fourth–third centuries B.C.E.)

Antisthenes, companion of Socrates and present at his death

Diogenes of Sinope, source of the Cynics' name, the "dog philosophers"; from *kyon* (dog)

Crates of Thebes, Diogenes' successor

Hipparchia of Maroneia

Later Figures of the Cynic Tradition

Dio Chrysostrom (circa 40–after 112 C.E.), *Orations* 4, 6, and 8–10.

Lucian of Samosata (circa 115–circa 200 C.E.), *Philosophers for Sale; Life of Demonax; Hermotimus, or Concerning the Sects; The Cynic* (Pseudo-Lucian).

See "A Comprehensive Catalogue of Known Cynic Philosophers," in *The Cynics: The Cynic Movement in Antiquity and Its Legacy,* ed. R. B. Branham and M.-O. Goulet-Cazé.

School of Isocrates (founded in Athens circa 392 B.C.E.)

Isocrates, Greek rhetorician, pupil of both Socrates and Gorgias, rival of Plato

Fourth-Century Hellenic Philosophy

Plato

Complete Works, ed. J. M. Cooper.

See especially *Republic* (trans. H. Bloom), *Symposium, Ion, Meno, Theatetus, Sophist, Parmenides, Timaeus*.

Plato in Twelve Volumes, Loeb Classical Library. Greek and English opposed pages.

Aristotle

The Complete Works of Aristotle, 2 vols., ed. J. Barnes.

See especially *Prior* and *Posterior Analytics, De Anima, Physics, Metaphysics, Nicomachean Ethics, Politics, Rhetoric, Poetics* (trans. J. Hutton).

Aristotle in Twenty-Three Volumes, Loeb Classical Library. Greek and English opposed pages.

Summaries

P. Shorey, *What Plato Said.*

W. D. Ross, *Aristotle: A Complete Exposition of His Works and Thought.*

Greek Academy (established by Plato circa 385 B.C.E.)

Old Academy (development of Platonic philosophy)

Heraclides of Pontus, temporary head of the Academy during Plato's third Sicilian journey

Speusippus, head of the Academy following Plato's death

Xenocrates, Speusippus's successor

Polemon of Athens, Xenocrates' successor

Crates of Athens, Polemon's successor

New Academy (debate with Stoicism; development of Skepticism)

See below, SKEPTICISM.

The Peripatetic School (founded by Aristotle circa 335 B.C.E.; name derived from a "covered walking hall" [*peripatos*] in the Lyceum)

Theophrastus, successor to Aristotle; *Characters.*

Strato of Lampsakos, successor to Theophrastus

Andronicus of Rhodes (first century B.C.E.), established the canon of Aristotle's works

Commentaries: Aristotle

Commentaries on Aristotle are collected in the Berlin *Commentaria in Aristotelem Graeca* (1882–1909), totaling about 15,000 pages. In the 1980s, under the general editorship of R. Sorabji, a project was begun to translate the most significant texts of these commentaries into English.

Among the most important Greek commentators on Aristotle in late antiquity is Alexander of Aphrodisias (fl. circa 200 C.E.), who taught in Athens; he exerted considerable influence on later Greek, Arabic, and Latin philosophy through the Renaissance.

MOVEMENTS OF HELLENISTIC AND ROMAN THOUGHT

Stoicism

Early Stoa (third century B.C.E.)

Zeno of Citium

Cleanthes of Assos, *Hymn to Zeus.*

Chrysippus of Soli

Middle Stoa (second and first centuries B.C.E.)

Diogenes of Seleucia

Panaetius of Rhodes

Posidonius of Apamea

Late Stoa (Roman; first and second centuries C.E.)

Seneca, *Moral Essays and Moral Letters.*

Epictetus, *Discourses* and *Manual.*

Marcus Aurelius, *Meditations.*

Epicureanism

Epicurus, *Epicurus: The Extant Remains,* ed. C. Bailey.

Philodemus of Gadara, *On Methods of Inference.*

Lucretius, *The Way Things Are: The De Rerum Natura,* trans. R. Humphries.

Skepticism

Academic Skepticism (third to first centuries B.C.E.)

New Academy (see above, GREEK ACADEMY)

Arcesilaus of Pitane, successor to Crates of the Old Academy

Carneades of Cyrene

Cleitomachus, successor to Carneades

Philo of Larisa, successor to Cleitomachus

Antiochus of Ascalon, last prominent member of the New Academy

Pyrrhonian Tradition (circa third century B.C.E. to third century C.E.)

Pyrrho of Elis

Timon of Phlius, student of Pyrrho

Aenesidemus

Sextus Empiricus, *Outlines of Pyrrhonism.*

See also *Sextus Empiricus: Selections from the Major Writings on Scepticism, Man, and God,* ed. P. Hallie.

Cicero

Marcus Tullius Cicero, *De Officiis (On Duties)*; *Tusculan Disputations; De Finibus (On Ends)*, ethical discussions, including criticism of Epicurean, Stoic, and Peripatetic doctrines; *De Natura Deorum; De Divinatione; De Fato,* Epicurean, Stoic, and Academic arguments about theology and natural philosophy; *Academica,* accounts of Hellenistic epistemological debates between dogmatic and skeptical views; *De Oratore,* book 1, on the relation of philosophy to rhetoric; *De Re Publica,* especially book 6, "The Dream of Scipio."

Collected Works

Cicero in Twenty-Eight Volumes, Loeb Classical Library. Latin and English opposed pages.

Biography

E. Rawson, *Cicero: A Portrait.*

Hellenistic Judaism

Philo Judaeus (circa 20 B.C.E.–40 C.E.), *Selections from Philo,* ed. H. Lewy.

Rhetorical Aesthetics

Longinus (late first century C.E.), *On the Sublime.*

Philosophy of Science and Medicine

Galen (129–circa 215 C.E.), *Three Treatises on the Nature of Science,* trans. R. Walzer and M. Frede.

Middle Platonism (late first and second centuries C.E.)

Plutarch, *Moralia.*

Apuleius, *Metamorphoses.*

Other figures: Albinus, Atticus, Numenius of Apamea

Neoplatonism

School of Plotinus

Plotinus, *Enneads.*

Porphry, *Porphyry the Phoenician: Isagoge,* trans. E. Warren; *On Aristotle's Categories,* trans. S. Strange.

Neoplatonic Philosophy, ed. J. Dillon and L. P. Gerson.

Syrian School

Iamblichus

School of Athens (closed by Justinian in 529 C.E.)

Plutarch of Athens, founder (circa 350–433 C.E.)

Proclus, *Elements of Theology, The Platonic Theology,* and commentaries on the Platonic dialogues.

Damascius, *On First Principles;* and commentaries on Aristotle and Plato.

Simplicius (studied with Ammonius in Alexandria); extensive commentaries on Aristotle.

See J. C. de Vogel, *Greek Philosophy,* vol. 3, selections of texts from Porphyry, Iamblichus, Proclus, and Damascius.

"Theurgic" School of Pergamum

Sallust, *Orations*.

Julian, *Orations*.

Alexandrian School

Hierocles (Plutarch's pupil), founder

Ammonius Saccas (early third century C.E.)

Hypatia (circa 370–415 C.E.), a Greek Neoplatonist who taught in Alexandria

For selections on Hellenistic philosophy, see B. Inwood and L. P. Gerson, *Hellenistic Philosophy: Introductory Readings*.

Roman Law

530 C.E.: *Corpus Iuris Civilis*: *The Digest of Justinian*, 2 vols., trans. and ed. A. Watson. See also the textbooks: *The Institutes of Justinian*, trans. J. A. C. Thomas; and *The Institutes of Gaius*, trans. W. M. Gordon and O. F. Robinson. Ulpian, in the first book of the *Digest* (1.1.10.2), suggests that jurisprudence is for the Romans what philosophy was for the Greeks (*sophia* becomes *iurisprudentia*). The law is the embodiment of divine and civil wisdom.

Commentaries: Ancient Philosophy

E. V. Arnold, *Roman Stoicism*.

C. Bailey, *The Greek Atomists and Epicurus*.

R. B. Branham and M.-O. Goulet-Cazé, eds., *The Cynics: The Cynic Movement in Antiquity and Its Legacy*.

Diogenes Laertius, *Lives of Eminent Philosophers*.

D. R. Dudley, *A History of Cynicism: From Diogenes to the Sixth Century*.

B. Farrington, *Greek Science*.

W. K. C. Guthrie, *A History of Greek Philosophy,* 6 vols.

P. Hadot, *What Is Ancient Philosophy?*

W. Jaeger, *Paideia: The Ideals of Greek Culture,* 3 vols.

J. Klein, *Greek Mathematical Thought and the Origin of Algebra.*

P. O. Kristeller, *Greek Philosophers of the Hellenistic Age.*

B. Mates, *Stoic Logic.*

G. Murray, *Five Stages of Greek Religion.*

B. Nicholas, *An Introduction to Roman Law.*

F. E. Peters, *Greek Philosophical Terms: A Historical Lexicon.*

J. M. Rist, *Stoic Philosophy.*

H. Spiegelberg, ed., *The Socratic Enigma.*

R. T. Wallis, *Neoplatonism,* 2nd ed.

T. Whittaker, *The Neo-Platonists.*

E. Zeller, *The Stoics, Epicureans, and Sceptics.*

Loeb Classical Library: the extant writings of many classical philosophers, including figures of the early medieval period, are available in the original, with opposed English translation, in the volumes of the Loeb Classical Library, Harvard University Press.

MEDIEVAL PHILOSOPHY

From the Council of Nicaea (325) to the Closing of the School of Athens (529) and the Fall of Constantinople (1453)

The Middle Ages dealt with man as a function of God, whose image he was thought to be: "Trinitarian psychologies" correspond to theologies of the Trinity; data from perception or from a rational analysis of the mind become part of a mental structure recalling that of the divine life. Sometimes remarkable for its precision and subtlety, this correspondence presupposes at least an implicit answer to questions like these: To what degree can the reflection of the human mind on itself enlighten it about the nature of its transcendent beginning? Or, by revealing Himself, does not a God who is said to have created men in His image disclose something of the most profound structure of their being, inaccessible to simple reflection? . . .

What characterizes the notion of Christian philosophy is an influence of Christianity on speculations that wish to be rational. This poses a graver problem for the believer than for the unbeliever. It is the former who, in order not to make void faith by destroying the transcendence of its object, must reject the extreme judgment of Lessing's formula: "Without doubt religious truths were not rational when they were revealed, but they were revealed in order to become so."

Whether dogmas are conceived in terms of a final judgment as principles of life or obstacles to be surmounted, the values they postulate and the adherence accorded to them—since they are not alone in man—give rise to interior conflicts that appear not only in unbelief but even in the bosom of faith. We touch here on a theological dimension of the Middle Ages which renders that age less remote and which, in fact, brings it very close to us. Too often the Middle Ages have been imagined as being perfectly organic, completely harmonious, and somewhat rigid; at the bottom of its intellectual life we find agitation, discord, and division; that is to say, conflicts of the profane order with the sacred, a dialogue between the human and the divine.

—Paul Vignaux, *Philosophy in the Middle Ages*

THE HISTORY OF PHILOSOPHY IN OUTLINE

(Selections from the works of philosophers cited in the Medieval section appear in R. McKeon, *Selections from Medieval Philosophers,* 2 vols.)

PATRISTIC AUTHORS

Greeks: (pre-Nicaean) Saint Irenaeus, Clement of Alexandria, Origen; (post-Nicaean) Saint Basil of Cesarea, Saint Gregory of Nyssa, Saint John Chrysostom

Latins (second to fifth centuries): Tertullian, Lactantius. Chief teachers of the Latin churches: Saint Ambrose, Saint Jerome, Saint Augustine, Saint Gregory the Great

EARLY MEDIEVAL PHILOSOPHERS

Saint Augustine, *Confessions; On the Trinity; City of God;* "On the Free Will" (McKeon).

Boethius, *Consolation of Philosophy;* "The Second Edition of the Commentaries on the *Isagoge* of Porphyry" (McKeon).

Isidore of Seville, *Etymologies.*

Carolingian Renaissance: Reign of Charlemagne (768–814). Classification of the seven liberal arts into the *quadrivium* (arithmetic, geometry, astronomy, music) and the *trivium* (grammar, rhetoric, dialectic). Alcuin (English); John Scotus Erigena (Irish), "On the Division of Nature" (McKeon); Paul Warnefrid (Lombard); Theodulf of Orleans (Spanish); Remigius of Auxerre (French); Rabanus Maurus (German).

Peter Abelard, *Ethical Writings,* trans. P. Spade; "The Glosses on Porphyry" (McKeon).

Debate on universals: see *Five Texts on the Medieval Problem of Universals: Porphyry, Boethius, Abelard, Duns Scotus, Ockham,* trans. P. Spade.

Saint Anselm of Canterbury, *Proslogion* and *Monologion*, trans.
T. Williams; "Dialogue on Truth" (McKeon).

The school of Chartres; John of Salisbury, *Metalogicon*, trans.
D. D. McGarry.

The school of St. Victor (Augustinian), founded by William of
Champeaux in 1108; Hugh of St. Victor, *Didascalicon*, trans.
J. Taylor.

Peter Lombard, *Book of Sentences* (book 1, "On the Trinity"; book
2, "On the Creation of Things"; book 3, "On the Incarnation";
book 4, "On the Doctrine of Signs [or Sacraments]"); "The
IV Books of Sentences" (McKeon).

ISLAMIC PHILOSOPHY (800–1400)

Abu Yusuf al-Kindī, *On First Philosophy*, trans. A. Ivry.

Abu Nasr al-Fārābi, *Al-Fārābi's Short Commentary on Aristotle's
Prior Analytics*, trans. N. Rescher.

Avicenna (Ibn Sīnā), *Avicenna on Theology*, trans. A. J. Arberry;
A Treatise on the Canon of Medicine, trans. O. C. Gruner;
Avicenna's Psychology, trans. F. Rahman.

Abū Hamid al-Ghazālī (critic of Avicenna), *Incoherence of the
Philosophers*, trans. S. A. Kamali.

Averroës (Ibn Rushd), commentaries on Aristotle; *The
Incoherence of the Incoherence* (reply to al-Ghazālī's *Incoherence
of the Philosophers*).

Avempace (Abu Bakr Ibn Bājja), *Tadbir al-Motawahhid* (treatise
on "The Role of the Solitary"), partial trans. D. M. Dunlop in
Journal of the Royal Asiatic Society (1945).

'Abdurrahmān Ibn Khaldūn, *The Muqaddima: An Introduction to
History*, trans. G. Rosenthal.

Classical Arabic Philosophy: An Anthology of Sources, trans.
J. McGinnis and D. C. Reisman.

For brief accounts of the transmission of the Aristotelian corpus
into the Latin world via Islamic culture, see F. Copleston,
A History of Philosophy, vol. 2, chap. 21; and D. L. O'Leary,
Arabic Thought and Its Place in History, chaps. 10 and 11.

JEWISH PHILOSOPHY (1000–1450)

Avicebron (Solomon Ibn Gabirol), *The Fountain of Life,* trans.
    H. E. Wedeck; *The Improvement of Moral Qualities,* trans.
    S. S. Wise.

Judah Halevi, *Book of the Kuzari,* trans. H. Hirschfeld.

Abraham Ibn Da'ud, *The Book of Tradition,* trans. G. Cohen;
    The Exalted Faith, trans. N. Samuelson.

Maimonides (Moses ben Maimon), *The Guide of the Perplexed,*
    trans. C. Rabin.

Gersonides (Levi ben Gershom), *The Wars of the Lord* (books
    1–4), trans. S. Feldman.

Hasdai Crescas, *Light of the Lord,* partial trans. H. A. Wolfson in
    Crescas' Critique of Aristotle.

Joseph Albo, *Sefer ha-'Ikkarim* (*The Book of Roots*), 5 vols., ed. and
    trans. I. Husik.

THIRTEENTH CENTURY:
THE "GOLDEN AGE" OF SCHOLASTICISM

Alexander of Hales. First to teach theology by lecturing on
    the *Sentences* of Peter Lombard; his emphasis on speculative
    theology initiated the golden age of Scholasticism.

Robert Grosseteste, "On Truth" and "The *Summa* of Philosophy"
    (the Pseudo-Grosseteste) (McKeon).

Saint Albert the Great, "The Short Natural Treatises on the
    Intellect and the Intelligible" (McKeon).

Roger Bacon, *Three Treatments of Universals,* trans. T. S. Maloney; "The "Opus Majus" (McKeon).

Siger of Brabant, *De Anima Intellectiva* (sustains Averroës' analysis of Aristotle's doctrine of the soul).

Saint Bonaventure, *The Journey of the Mind to God,* trans. P. Boehner; "Commentary on the Four Books of *Sentences* of Peter Lombard" (McKeon).

After 1255, works of Aristotle officially admitted into the curriculum of the University of Paris. (*Summa Theologiae* written by Thomas Aquinas circa 1266–73.)

Thomas Aquinas

Saint Thomas Aquinas, *Summa Contra Gentiles,* 4 vols.; and *Summa Theologiae,* 22 vols., trans. by the Fathers of the English Dominican Province; *On Being and Essence,* 2nd ed., trans. A. Maurer; "The Disputed Questions on Truth" (McKeon).

See *Basic Writings of Saint Thomas Aquinas,* 2 vols., ed. A. C. Pegis; *Treatise on Human Nature* (*Summa Theologiae,* 1a75–89), trans. R. Pasnou.

Treatise on Law (*Summa Theologiae,* Questions 90–97), trans. R. J. Regan.

Later Medieval Philosophers

Ramon Lull, *Tree of Knowledge; Ars Brevis; Ars Generalis Ultima.* See *Selected Works of Ramon Lull,* trans. A. Bonner.

Matthew of Aquasparta, "Ten Disputed Questions on Knowledge" (McKeon).

Meister (Johannes) Eckhart, *Meister Eckhart: A Modern Translation,* trans. R. B. Blakney; *Selected Treatises and Sermons,* trans. J. M. Clark and J. V. Skinner.

John Duns Scotus, *Duns Scotus: Philosophical Writings,* trans.
   A. Wolter; "The Oxford Commentary on the Four Books of
   the Master of the Sentence" (McKeon).

Marsilius of Padua, *The Defender of Peace: The Defensor Pacis,*
   trans. A. Gewirth.

William of Ockham, *Ockham: Philosophical Writings,* trans.
   P. Boehner; "The Seven Quodlibeta" (McKeon).

Jean Buridan, *Jean Buridan's Logic: The Treatise on Supposition; The
   Treatise on Consequences,* trans. P. King; *Sophisms on Meaning
   and Truth,* trans. T. K. Scott.

Oxford calculators: *Liber Calculationum* (written before 1350),
   natural philosophers, mathematicians, and logicians (Walter
   Burley, Roger Swineshead, John Bode).

Nicholas Oresme, *Le Livre du Ciel et du Monde,* ed. A. D.
   Menut and A. J. Denomy (edition and English translation of
   Oresme's French translation of and commentary on Aristotle's
   On the Heavens).

Commentaries: Medieval Philosophy

A. H. Armstrong, ed., *The Cambridge History of Later Greek and
   Early Medieval Philosophy.*

H. von Campenhausen, *The Fathers of the Latin Church.*

F. Copleston, *A History of Philosophy,* vols. 2 and 3.

T. J. De Boer, *The History of Philosophy in Islam.*

M. De Wulf, *History of Medieval Philosophy,* 2 vols.

E. Gilson, *History of Christian Philosophy in the Middle Ages.*

C. H. Haskins, *Studies in the History of Medieval Science.*

J. Huizinga, *The Waning of the Middle Ages.*

I. Husik, *History of Medieval Jewish Philosophy.*

D. Knowles, *Evolution of Medieval Thought.*

N. Kretzmann, A. Kenny, and J. Pinborg, eds., *Cambridge History of Later Medieval Philosophy: From the Rediscovery of Aristotle to the Disintegration of Scholasticism, 1100–1600.*

M. W. Laistner, *Thought and Letters in Western Europe A.D. 500–900.*

R. Lerner and M. Mahdi, eds., *Medieval Political Philosophy: A Sourcebook.*

A. D. Nock, *Early Gentile Christianity and Its Hellenistic Background.*

D. L. O'Leary, *Arabic Thought and Its Place in History.*

N. Rescher, *Studies in the History of Arabic Logic.*

D. E. Sharp, *Franciscan Philosophy at Oxford in the Thirteenth Century.*

R. W. Southern, *The Making of the Middle Ages.*

H. O. Taylor, *The Classical Heritage of the Middle Ages.*

W. Threadgold, *Renaissances Before the Renaissance: Cultural Revivals of Late Antiquity and the Middle Ages.*

P. Vignaux, *Philosophy in the Middle Ages: An Introduction.*

R. Walzer, *Greek into Arabic.*

RENAISSANCE PHILOSOPHY

From 1350 to the Early Seventeenth Century

The philosophy of the early Renaissance does not seem to bear out Hegel's presupposition that the full consciousness and spiritual essence of an epoch is contained in its philosophy; that philosophy, as self-conscious awareness of consciousness itself, reflects—as the proper focus of the period—the entire manifold of the age. At the end of the thirteenth and the beginning of the fourteenth century, a new life begins to stir in poetry, in the visual arts, in politics, and in historical life, becoming ever stronger and even more conscious of itself as a movement of spiritual renewal. But at first glance, the new spirit seems to find neither expression nor echo in the philosophical thought of the time. For, even at those points where it seems to be freeing itself from the findings of Scholasticism, the philosophy of the early Renaissance remains bound to the general *forms* of Scholastic thought.

The attack Petrarch ventures in his *De sui ipsius et multorum ignorantia* ["On His Own Ignorance and That of Many Others"] against the philosophy of the Schools is in fact only a witness to the unbroken force which that philosophy still exercises upon the time. Indeed, the principle that Petrarch opposes to the Scholastic and Aristotelian doctrine has neither philosophical origin nor content. It is not a new method of thought; rather, it is the new cultural ideal of "eloquence." Henceforth, Aristotle will and may no longer be considered the master of knowledge, the representative of "culture" pure and simple, for his works—those that have come down to us—contain "not the slightest trace of eloquence." Humanist criticism, then, turns against the style, not against the content of Aristotle's works. But this criticism gradually annihilates its own premises. For, as the scope of humanist knowledge broadens, and as its scholarly instruments become sharper and finer, the picture of the Scholastic Aristotle must necessarily give way to the picture of the true Aristotle, which can now be drawn from the sources themselves. Leonardo Bruni, the first translator of the *Politics* and the *Nicomachean Ethics,* asserted that Aristotle himself would not have recognized his own works in the transformation they had undergone at the hands of the Scholastics, just as Actaeon was not recognized by his own dogs after he had been changed into a deer.

—Ernst Cassirer, *The Individual and the Cosmos in Renaissance Philosophy*

(Selections from the works of philosophers cited in the Renaissance section are from E. Cassirer, P. O. Kristeller, and J. H. Randall, eds., *The Renaissance Philosophy of Man;* and A. B. Fallico and H. Shapiro, eds., *Renaissance Philosophy,* 2 vols.)

THE ITALIAN PHILOSOPHERS

Renaissance Humanism

Francesco Petrarch, "On His Own Ignorance and That of Many Others" (Cassirer); "On the Remedies of Good and Bad Fortune" (Fallico and Shapiro).

Leon Battista Alberti, *Momus,* trans. Sarah Knight; "Three Dialogues" (Fallico and Shapiro).

Lorenzo Valla, *On Pleasure: De Voluptate,* trans. M. Lorch and A. K. Hieatt; "Dialogue on Free Will" (Cassirer; also Fallico and Shapiro).

Gianozzo Manetti, "On the Dignity and Excellence of Man" (Fallico and Shapiro).

For the humanist conception of education (*studia humanitatis*), see the essays of Vergerio, Bruni, Piccolomini, and Guarino in *Humanist Educational Treatises,* ed. and trans. Craig W. Kallendorf.

Renaissance Platonism

Marsilio Ficino, *The Letters of Marsilio Ficino,* trans. by members of the Language Department of the School of Economic Science, London; *Commentary on Plato's Symposium on Love,* trans. S. Jayne; *Platonic Theology,* 5 vols., trans. M. J. B. Allen; "Five Questions Concerning the Mind" (Cassirer); "Concerning the Sun" (Fallico and Shapiro).

Platonic Academy of Florence (1462–1494): circle of scholars
gathered around Marsilio Ficino, under the auspices of
the Medici, and including Giovanni Pico della Mirandola,
Cristoforo Landino, Lorenzo de' Medici, and Angelo
Poliziano (see Poliziano, *Silvae,* ed. and trans. Charles
Fantazzi).

Giovanni Pico della Mirandola, "Oration on the Dignity of Man"
(Cassirer; also Fallico and Shapiro).

Gianfrancesco Pico della Mirandola, *On the Imagination* (Latin-
English), trans. H. Caplan.

Leone Ebreo, "On Love and Desire"; "A Dialogue Between
Philo and Sophia" (Fallico and Shapiro).

Giulio Camillo, *L'idea del theatro* (*The Idea of the Theatre*),
trans. in Lu Berry Wenneker, "An Examination of *L'idea del
theatro* of Giulio Camillo" (Ph.D. dissertation, University of
Pittsburgh, 1970).

Renaissance Aristotelianism

Pietro Pomponazzi, "On the Immortality of the Soul" (Cassirer);
"On God's Foreknowledge and Human Freedom" (Fallico and
Shapiro).

Jacopo Zabarella, *Opera Logica,* and commentaries on Aristotle's
Physics and *De Anima.*

Torquato Tasso, "On the Art of Poetry" (Fallico and Shapiro).

Political, Moral, and Natural Philosophy

Niccolò Machiavelli, *The Prince* and *The Discourses.* See
Machiavelli: The Chief Works and Others, 3 vols., trans.
A. Gilbert.

Bernardino Telesio, "On the Nature of Things According to
Their Own Proper Principles" (Fallico and Shapiro).

Tommaso Campanella, *The City of the Sun: A Poetical Dialogue,* trans. D. J. Donno; "On the Sense and Feeling in All Things and on Magic" (Fallico and Shapiro).

Giordano Bruno, *On the Infinite Universe and Worlds,* in D. W. Singer, *Giordano Bruno: His Life and Thought;* and *The Expulsion of the Triumphant Beast,* trans. A. D. Imerti.

THE TRANSALPINE THINKERS

Germany, Switzerland, and the Low Countries

Nicholas of Cusa, *Of Learned Ignorance,* trans. J. Hopkins; *The Vision of God,* trans. E. G. Salter; *The Idiot,* trans. W. R. Dennes.

Johannes Reuchlin, "On the Cabalistic Art" (Fallico and Shapiro).

Desiderius Erasmus, *The Praise of Folly.* See also *The Erasmus Reader,* ed. E. Rulmmel; "On the Philosophy of Christ" (Fallico and Shapiro).

Ulrich von Hutten, "Eight Letters of Obscure Men" (Fallico and Shapiro).

Henricus Cornelius Agrippa von Nettesheim (alchemist), *De Occulta Philosophia;* "On the Uncertainty of Our Knowledge" (Fallico and Shapiro).

Paracelsus (Philippus Aureolus Theophrastus Bombastus von Hohenheim; alchemist), *Selected Writings,* ed. J. Jacobi, trans. N. Guterman.

Justus Lipsius, "On Constancy" (Fallico and Shapiro).

Jakob Boehme, *Six Theosophic Points and Other Writings,* trans. J. R. Earle; *The 'Key' of Jacob Boehme,* trans. W. Law.

Protestant Reformation

Martin Luther, "To the Christian Nobility of the German
Nation"; "The Babylonian Captivity of the Church"; "The
Freedom of a Christian," from vols. 31, 36, and 44 of the
American edition of *Luther's Works,* ed. H. T. Lehmann.

France

Jacques Lefèvre d'Étaples, "On Translating the Gospels into
French" (Fallico and Shapiro).

Petrus Ramus, "Thoughts About Aristotle" (Fallico and
Shapiro).

Jean Bodin, *Method for the Easy Comprehension of History,* trans.
B. Reynolds; *The Colloquium of the Seven About Secrets of the
Sublime,* trans. M. L. D. Kuntz.

Michel de Montaigne, *The Complete Works of Montaigne,* trans.
D. M. Frame.

Pierre Charron, "Concerning Wisdom" (Fallico and Shapiro).

Guillaume du Vair, "The Moral Philosophy of the Stoics"
(Fallico and Shapiro).

Spain

Juan Luis Vives, "A Fable About Man" (Cassirer); "Two
Dialogues on Education" (Fallico and Shapiro).

Saint John of the Cross, "Concerning the Direction of
Contemplative Souls" (Fallico and Shapiro).

Francisco Suárez, *Metaphysical Disputations* (Disputations 5,
6, 7, 10, 11, 17, 18, 19, 22 [partial], 31, and 54 have been
translated by various scholars and have appeared with various
publishers); *Selections from Three Works of Francisco Suárez,*
trans. G. L. Williams and others (Classics of International
Law, No. 20); "Man Acts Freely" (Fallico and Shapiro). Suàrez
is often regarded as the last major figure of Scholasticism.

Baltasar Gracián y Morales, *The Art of Worldly Wisdom,* trans.
C. Mauere.

England

John Colet, "On Pagan Philosophy and the Ninefold Order of
Being" (Fallico and Shapiro).

Thomas More, *Utopia.* See vol. 4 of *The Complete Works of St.
Thomas More,* ed. R. S. Sylvester.

Francis Bacon, *New Organon; The Advancement of Learning;
New Atlantis.* See *The Works of Francis Bacon,* 14 vols., ed.
J. Spedding, R. L. Ellis, and D. D. Heath.

Commentaries: Renaissance Philosophy

W. Bouwsma, *The Waning of the Renaissance 1550–1640.*

J. Burckhardt, *The Civilization of the Renaissance in Italy.*

E. Cassirer, *The Individual and the Cosmos in Renaissance
Philosophy.*

B. Copenhaver and C. B. Schmitt, *Renaissance Philosophy.*

A. Field, *The Origins of the Platonic Academy in Florence.*

D. Freedberg, *The Eye of the Lynx: Galileo, His Friends, and the
Beginnings of Modern Natural History.*

E. Garin, *Italian Humanism: Philosophy and Civic Life in the
Renaissance.*

E. Grassi, *Renaissance Humanism: Studies in Philosophy and
Poetics.*

J. Hankins, *Plato in the Italian Renaissance.*

P. O. Kristeller, *Eight Philosophers of the Italian Renaissance.*

A. W. Levi, *Humanism and Politics: Studies in the Relationship of
Power and Value in the Western Tradition.*

R. Popkin, *The History of Scepticism from Erasmus to Descartes.*

J. H. Randall, *The School of Padua and the Emergence of Modern Science.*

P. Rossi, *Logic and the Art of Memory: The Quest for a Universal Language (Clavis Universalis).*

C. B. Schmitt, *Aristotle and the Renaissance.*

C. B. Schmitt and Q. Skinner, eds., *The Cambridge History of Renaissance Philosophy.*

H. O. Taylor, *Thought and Expression in the Sixteenth Century.*

F. A. Yates, *The Art of Memory.*

I Tatti Renaissance Library: the writings of many Renaissance figures, both literary and philosophical, are available in the original Latin with opposed English translation in the volumes prepared by the I Tatti Renaissance Library, Harvard University Press. These are similar in format to the volumes of the Loeb Classical Library (see page 36). The first volumes appeared in 2001, and more volumes are being added regularly.

MODERN PHILOSOPHY

From Descartes' *Discourse* (1637) to the Death of Nietzsche (1900) and the Movements of the Twentieth Century

Western man looks back with longing to two great periods of cultural synthesis—the secular millennium of the Athenian city state and the other-worldly paradise of the Middle Ages. . . .

The ancient and the mediaeval world possess a picture of the human individual *which is not in doubt.* For almost two thousand years of history Western man seems to have known what his own nature is.

But sometime between the fourteenth and the seventeenth century (between the time of Nicholas of Cusa and of Descartes) this ceases to be true. The change can be stated in a somewhat different way. In distinguishing between ancient and mediaeval philosophy on the one hand, and modern philosophy beginning with Bacon or Descartes on the other, it has sometimes been asserted that the former was primarily metaphysical while the latter has been more and more epistemological. The ancient and mediaeval thinkers were concerned with "things." The moderns have been more concerned with "how things are known." To the Greeks, man's nature presented no particular problems; but the world of nature and its genesis was a source of constant preoccupation and of doubt. To a discriminating reader Greek ethics (the *Nicomachean Ethics* or Plato's *Republic* perhaps) seems almost *descriptive* in its assurance, while Greek physics and Greek cosmology (the *Physics* or the *Timaeus*) have a tentative and *speculative* character.

From the time of the European Renaissance this situation has been reversed. Throughout the seventeenth century—"the century of genius" as Whitehead calls it—from the time of Kepler and Galileo to the time of Newton, Huygens, and Leibniz the world of physical nature was being made secure. The spatial relations of matter were given mathematical values; physical process was brought under such control that physics could be conceived as a demonstrative science. Therefore Newton's *Principia* is written on the geometrical model of Euclid's *Elements*.

But at the very moment when the success of the science of the physical world is most assured, the status of the human mind through which that science had been obtained begins to be in doubt. It is not only Immanuel Kant who asks in his *Critique of Pure Reason,* How is the science of nature possible? What is the character of that human understanding which gives us physical science? All of the philosophers from Bacon to Hegel, and particularly those British thinkers following in the wake of Newton—Locke, Berkeley, and Hume—take as their fundamental point of departure this very question. Because the mind is the agency of natural understanding, its nature has become the center of the philosophical battleground. "But what, then, am I?" asks Descartes. "A thinking thing, it has been said. But what is a thinking thing?"

—Albert William Levi, *Philosophy and the Modern World*

EARLY MODERN PHILOSOPHIES
AND PHILOSOPHICAL SYSTEMS

The Continent

René Descartes, *Rules for the Direction of the Mind; Discourse on
Method; Meditations on First Philosophy; Principles of Philosophy;
The Passions of the Soul.* See *The Philosophical Writings of
Descartes,* 3 vols., trans. J. Cottingham, R. Stoothoff, D.
Murdoch; and *Oeuvres de Descartes,* 11 vols., ed. C. Adam and
P. Tannery. Paris: Vrin. Paperback edition, 1996.

Marin Mersenne, compiler of *Objections* to Descartes'
Meditations.

Galileo Galilei, *The Assayer,* in *Discoveries and Opinions of Galileo,*
abridged, trans. S. Drake.

Pierre Gassendi, *The Selected Works of Pierre Gassendi,* trans.
C. Brush.

Blaise Pascal, *Pensées.*

Antoine Arnauld and Pierre Nicole, *Port-Royal Logic.* See *Logic,
or The Art of Thinking,* trans. and ed. J. V. Buroker.

Nicolas Malebranche, *The Search After Truth: Elucidations of
the Search After Truth,* trans. T. Lennon and P. J. Olscamp;
Philosophical Selections, ed. S. Nadler.

Hugo Grotius, *The Law of War and Peace,* trans. F. W. Kelsey.

Robert Boyle, *Selected Philosophical Papers of Robert Boyle,* ed.
M. A. Stewart.

Benedict de Spinoza, *Ethics; On the Improvement of the
Understanding; Theologico-Political Treatise,* in *The Chief Works
of Benedict de Spinoza,* 2 vols., trans. R. H. M. Elwes; *Earlier
Philosophical Writings,* trans. F. A. Hayes. See also *The Collected
Works of Spinoza,* ed. and trans. E. Curley (vol. 1, *Ethics*).

Gottfried Wilhelm Leibniz, *Monadology; Discourse on
Metaphysics; Theodicy.* See *Leibniz: Philosophical Essays,*

trans. R. Ariew and D. Garber. See also *Theodicy,* trans. E. M. Hubbard; *Philosophical Papers and Letters,* trans. L. E. Loemker; *Leibniz and Clarke: Correspondence,* ed. R. Ariew.

Christian Wolff, *Preliminary Discourse on Philosophy in General,* trans. R. J. Blackwell.

Emanuel Swedenborg, *Heavenly Secrets (Arcano Coelestia),* 12 vols., trans. J. F. Potts. Swedenborg had a wide influence and was of interest to Emerson, Jaspers, and Kant. See Kant's satirical "review" of *Arcano Coelestia,* "Dreams of a Spirit-Seer," in *Kant on Swedenborg and Other Writings,* ed. G. R. Johnson.

Great Britain and Ireland

Cambridge Platonism (1630s–1680s): Benjamin Whichcote, Henry More, Ralph Cudworth, and John Smith, among others; they influenced Shaftesbury. Cudworth coined the term "Cartesianism" in 1662. See selections in *The Cambridge Platonists,* ed. E. T. Campagnac.

Thomas Hobbes, *Leviathan; De Cive.* See *English Works of Thomas Hobbes,* 11 vols., ed. W. Molesworth.

John Locke, *An Essay Concerning Human Understanding; Two Treatises of Government; A Letter Concerning Toleration.* See *The Works of John Locke,* 10 vols., ed. T. Tegg and others; *The Clarendon Edition of The Works of John Locke,* 1975–.

Isaac Newton, *Newton: A Norton Critical Edition,* ed. I. B. Cohen and R. S. Westfall.

George Berkeley, *A Treatise Concerning the Principles of Human Knowledge; An Essay Towards a New Theory of Vision; Three Dialogues Between Hylas and Philonous.* See *The Works of George Berkeley, Bishop of Cloyne,* 8 vols., ed. A. A. Luce and T. E. Jessop.

David Hume, *A Treatise of Human Nature; Enquiry Concerning Human Understanding; Enquiry Concerning the Principles of*

Morals; Dialogues Concerning Natural Religion. See *Hume's Philosophical Works,* 4 vols., ed. T. H. Green and T. H. Grose.

Thomas Reid, *An Inquiry into the Human Mind on the Principles of Common Sense.* See *Works,* 2 vols., ed. W. Hamilton.

Scottish common sense philosophy: founded by Thomas Reid, initially popularized by Dugald Stewart, and widely taught as a manner of philosophizing in Great Britain and the United States into the late nineteenth century.

ENLIGHTENMENT AND COUNTER-ENLIGHTENMENT THOUGHT

Pierre Bayle, *Dictionnaire Historique et Critique: Selections from Bayle's Dictionary,* ed. E. A. Beller and M. duP. Lee Jr. See also *The Historical and Critical Dictionary,* selective trans. R. Popkin and C. Brush.

Giambattista Vico, *The New Science,* trans. T. G. Bergin and M. H. Fisch; *Autobiography,* trans. M. H. Fisch and T. G. Bergin; *On the Study Methods of Our Time,* trans. E. Gianturco; *On the Most Ancient Wisdom of the Italians,* trans. L. M. Palmer. *Universal Law* (the full text is published in the following parts): "Synopsis of Universal Law" (trans. D. P. Verene), "On the One Principle and One End of Universal Law," "On the Constancy of the Jurisprudent," and "Dissertations" (trans. J. D. Schaeffer), *New Vico Studies* 21, 23, and 24 (2003, 2005, and 2006).

Bernard Mandeville, *The Fable of the Bees,* 2 vols., ed. F. B. Kaye.

Shaftesbury (Anthony Ashley Cooper, Third Earl of), *Characteristics of Men, Manners, Opinions, Times,* 2 vols., ed. J. M. Robertson; see especially "*Sensus Communis:* An Essay on the Freedom of Wit and Humour."

Baron de Montesquieu, *Spirit of the Laws,* trans. T. Nugent.

Voltaire (François-Marie Arouet), *Philosophical Dictionary,*
2 vols., trans. P. Gay; *Candide and Related Texts,* trans.
D. Wootton.

Francis Hutcheson, *An Inquiry into the Original of Our Ideas of
Beauty and Virtue, in Two Treatises.*

Julien Offray de La Mettrie, *Man a Machine and Man a Plant,*
trans. R. Watson and M. Rybalka.

Samuel Johnson, *The History of Rasselas, Prince of Abissinia,* ed.
Lynne Meloccano.

Jean-Jacques Rousseau, *First and Second Discourses,* trans. R. D.
Masters and J. R. Masters; *Social Contract,* ed. R. D. Masters,
trans. J. R. Masters; *Émile,* trans. A. Bloom; *Essay on the
Origin of Languages,* trans. A. Gourevitch.

Denis Diderot, general editor of the *Encyclopédie.* See *Selected
Works of Diderot,* trans. L. G. Crocker; *Rameau's Nephew and
Other Works,* trans. J. Barzun and R. H. Bowen.

Jean Le Rond d'Alembert, coeditor of the *Encyclopédie.* See
Preliminary Discourse to the Encyclopedia, trans. R. N. Schwab.

The *Encyclopédie* and *Les Philosophes.* Full English title,
*Encyclopedia, or a Descriptive Dictionary of the Sciences, Arts,
and Trades,* was published in 28 volumes from 1751 to 1772,
was edited by Diderot and d'Alembert, and contained 17,818
articles. According to Diderot, the purpose of an encyclopedia
"is to collect the knowledge dispersed on the surface of the
earth, and to unfold its general system." The *Encyclopédie*
fostered criticism in political, scientific, and theological
matters, vindicated experimental reason, and endorsed the
development of new sciences. Contributions were made to the
work by experts in all fields theoretical and applied. Many of
the contributors to the *Encyclopédie* were the philosophes, who
were men of letters, journalists, and intellectuals of the salon
culture of the eighteenth-century French Enlightenment.
The philosophes were philosophical thinkers but not

authors of philosophical systems in a traditional sense.
Among the famous philosophes who contributed articles
to the *Encyclopédie* were Voltaire, Rousseau, Montesquieu,
and d'Holbach. The tradition of the philosophes in French
philosophy goes back to Bodin in the sixteenth century
through Bayle in the seventeenth century and to Montesquieu
and the Encyclopedists in the eighteenth century.

Claude-Adrien Helvétius, *De L'Homme,* 2 vols. See *A Treatise
on Man: His Intellectual Faculties and His Education,* trans.
W. Hooper (1777; not a wholly reliable translation).

Étienne Bonnot de Condillac, *Treatise on the Sensations,* ed.
H. W. Carr, trans. G. Carr.

Adam Smith, *The Wealth of Nations.*

Paul-Henri Thiry d'Holbach, *The System of Nature,* trans.
H. D. Robinson.

Gotthold Ephraim Lessing, *Laocöon,* trans. E. A. McCormick;
Nathan the Wise; Lessing's Theological Writings, ed. and trans.
H. Chadwick.

Adam Ferguson, *An Essay on the History of Civil Society.*

Edmund Burke, *Reflections on the Revolution in France,* ed.
J. G. A. Pocock; *Philosophical Inquiry into the Origin of Our
Ideas on the Sublime and the Beautiful.*

Moses Mendelssohn, *Philosophical Writings,* trans. D. O.
Dahlstrom.

Johann Georg Hamann, *J. G. Hamann, with Selections from
His Writings,* ed. R. G. Smith.

Marquis de Condorcet, *Sketch for a Historical Tableau of the
Progress of the Human Mind,* ed. S. Hampshire, trans.
J. P. Barraclough.

Johann Gottfried Herder, *Outlines of a Philosophy of the History
of Man,* 2 vols., trans T. O. Churchill.

Jeremy Bentham, *An Introduction to the Principles of Morals and Legislation.*

British moral philosophy: see L. A. Selby-Bigge, ed., *British Moralists, Being Selections from Writers Principally of the Eighteenth Century,* 2 vols. Includes, among others, Joseph Butler, Samuel Clarke, Richard Price, John Brown, John Gay, William Paley.

Commentaries: Seventeenth and Eighteenth Centuries

E. N. da C. Andrada, *Science in the Seventeenth Century.*

C. L. Becker, *Heavenly City of the Eighteenth-Century Philosophers.*

I. Berlin, *Three Critics of the Enlightenment: Vico, Hamann, Herder,* ed. H. Hardy.

E. A. Burtt, *The Metaphysical Foundations of Modern Science.*

J. B. Bury, *The Idea of Progress.*

H. Butterfield, *The Origins of Modern Science.*

E. Cassirer, *The Philosophy of the Enlightenment.*

———, *The Platonic Renaissance in England.*

G. Clive, *The Romantic Enlightenment.*

L. Dupré, *The Enlightenment and the Intellectual Foundations of Modern Culture.*

C. W. Eliot, *English Philosophers of the Seventeenth and Eighteenth Century.*

J. W. Gough, *The Social Contract: A Critical Study of Its Development.*

P. Hazard, *European Thought in the Eighteenth Century.*

L. Lévy-Bruhl, *History of Modern Philosophy in France.*

F. Manuel, *The Eighteenth Century Confronts the Gods.*

C. R. Morris, *Locke, Berkeley, Hume.*

Steven Nadler, ed., *A Companion to Early Modern Philosophy.*

A. S. Pringle-Pattison, *Scottish Philosophy: A Comparison of the Scottish and German Answers to Hume.*

P. Rossi, *The Dark Abyss of Time: A History of the Earth and the History of Nations from Hooke to Vico.*

L. Stephen, *History of English Thought in the Eighteenth Century,* 2 vols.

A. Wolf, *A History of Science, Technology, and Philosophy in the 16th and 17th Centuries,* 2 vols.; and *in the 18th Century,* 2 vols.

GERMAN IDEALISM AND NINETEENTH-CENTURY PHILOSOPHY

Immanuel Kant

Critique of Pure Reason; Critique of Practical Reason; Critique of Judgment.
Werke, 10 vols. Darmstadt: Wissenschaftliche Buchgesellschaft.

Summary
E. Cassirer, *Kant's Life and Work.*

Georg Wilhelm Friedrich Hegel

Phenomenology of Spirit; Science of Logic; Encyclopaedia of Philosophical Sciences in Outline; Philosophy of Right.
Werke, 20 vols., and *Register.* Frankfurt am Main: Suhrkamp.

Summary
J. N. Findlay, *Hegel: A Re-Examination.*

Young Hegelians

The Young Hegelians (1830s and 1840s) were Hegel's immediate followers, such as D. F. Strauss, Ludwig Feuerbach, Bruno Bauer, and Arnold Ruge. See also Max Stirner, *The Ego and His Own*, trans. S. T. Byington. The Young Hegelians were often characterized as "right" and "left" Hegelians, the most famous left Hegelian being Karl Marx in his early years. See *The Young Hegelians: An Anthology*, ed. L. S. Stepelevich.

Johann Christian Friedrich Hölderlin, *Friedrich Hölderlin: Hyperion and Selected Poems*, ed. E. L. Santer.

Friedrich Heinrich Jacobi, *The Main Philosophical Writings and the Novel "Allwill,"* ed. and trans. G. di Giovanni.

Johann Gottlieb Fichte, *The Science of Knowledge* (*Wissenschaftslehre*), trans. P. Heath and J. Lachs; *Introductions to the Wissenschaftslehre and Other Writings (1797–1800)*, trans. D. Breazeale; *The Vocation of Man*, trans. P. Preuss.

Friedrich Schiller, *On the Aesthetic Education of Man in a Series of Letters*, trans. E. M. Wilkinson and L. A. Willoughby.

Friedrich Daniel Ernst Schleiermacher, *On Religion: Speeches to Its Cultured Despisers*, trans. R. Crouter.

Novalis, *Philosophical Writings*, trans. and ed. M. M. Stoljar.

Friedrich Wilhelm Joseph von Schelling, *System of Transcendental Idealism*, trans. P. Heath; *Bruno, or On the Natural and the Divine Principle of Things*, ed. and trans. M. G. Vater; *Of Human Freedom*, trans. J. Gutmann; *The Ages of the World*, trans. F. de W. Bolman.

Arthur Schopenhauer, *The World as Will and Representation*, 2 vols., trans. E. F. J. Payne; *On the Fourfold Root of the Principle of Sufficient Reason*, trans. E. F. J. Payne.

Auguste Comte, *The Positive Philosophy of Auguste Comte*, 2 vols., trans. and ed. H. Martineau (condensation of the *Cours de Philosophie Positive*, 6 vols.).

Ludwig Andreas Feuerbach, *The Essence of Christianity*, trans.
M. Evans; *Principles of the Philosophy of the Future*, trans.
M. Vogel.

John Stuart Mill, *John Stuart Mill's Philosophy of Scientific Method*, ed. E. Nagel (Mill's *A System of Logic*); *The Six Great Humanistic Essays of John Stuart Mill*, ed. A. W. Levi (includes *On Liberty* and *Utilitarianism*).

Søren Aabye Kierkegaard, *Either/Or: A Fragment of Life; Philosophical Fragments, or A Fragment of Philosophy*, trans.
D. F. Swenson; *Concluding Unscientific Postscript*, trans.
D. F. Swenson, L. M. Swenson, and W. Lowrie.

Karl Marx, *The Economic and Philosophical Manuscripts*, in *Early Writings*, ed. L. Coletti; *The Grundrisse*, ed. and trans. D. McLellan; *The Communist Manifesto* (with F. Engels); *Capital*, trans. B. Foukes. See also *Selected Writings*, ed. D. McLellan.

Charles Darwin, *On the Origin of Species*.

Herbert Spencer, *First Principles*.

Vladimir Sergeyevich Solovyov, *Lectures on Godmanhood*, trans.
P. Zouboff; *The Meaning of Love*, trans. J. Marshall.

Friedrich Nietzsche, *On the Genealogy of Morality*, trans. M. Clark and A. Swenson; *Beyond Good and Evil*, trans. W. Kaufmann; *Thus Spake Zarathustra* and *The Twilight of the Idols*, trans. W. Kaufmann in *The Portable Nietzsche; The Birth of Tragedy*, trans. W. Kaufmann and R. J. Hollingdale; *Schopenhauer as Educator*, trans. J. W. Hillesheim and M. R. Simpson.

Commentaries: Nineteenth Century

W. J. Brazill, *The Young Hegelians*.

C. Brinton, *English Political Thought in the Nineteenth Century*.

E. Cassirer, *The Problem of Knowledge: Philosophy, Science, and History Since Hegel*.

B. Feldman and R. D. Richardson, eds., *The Rise of Modern Mythology 1680–1860.*

S. Hook, *From Hegel to Marx.*

K. Löwith, *From Hegel to Nietzsche: The Revolution in Nineteenth-Century Thought.*

G. H. Mead, *Movements of Thought in the Nineteenth Century.*

J. T. Merz, *History of European Thought in the Nineteenth Century.*

R. Metz, *A Hundred Years of British Philosophy.*

J. Royce, *Lectures on Modern Idealism.*

———, *The Spirit of Modern Philosophy.*

H. Schnädelbach, *Philosophy in Germany 1831–1933.*

L. Stephen, *The English Utilitarians,* 3 vols.

PHILOSOPHIES FROM THE TURN OF THE CENTURY TO THE MID-TWENTIETH CENTURY

There is in the climate of the modern world a sense of impending disaster, a rootlessness of the person, a pervasive tenseness which points to certainties dissolved and emotional centers displaced. It is not accidental that the two most novel philosophic positions of the time—Logical Empiricism and Existentialism—should contribute to this massive effect—the one by narrowing the region of authentic knowledge to a point where it is no longer adequate to the breadth of human concern, the other elevating into ontological principles the human emotions of care, anxiety, anguish, abandonment, and despair.

—Albert William Levi, *Philosophy and the Modern World*

Two Early American Movements

New England transcendentalists (1836–60): Ralph Waldo
Emerson, *Essays;* Henry David Thoreau, *Walden;*
Amos Bronson Alcott, *Journals;* and others. See *The
Transcendentalist: An Anthology,* ed. P. Miller.

St. Louis Hegelians (after 1865): W. T. Harris, Henry L.
Brockmeyer, Thomas Davidson, George H. Howison,
Denton J. Snider, Adolf E. Kroeger, Ann C. Brackett. They
founded the St. Louis Philosophical Society (1866) and the
Journal of Speculative Philosophy (1867–93), the first American
philosophical journal. See *The St. Louis Hegelians,* 3 vols.
(selected writings), ed. M. H. DeArmey and J. A. Good. The
St. Louis movement was preceded by several years by a group
of Cincinnati (Ohio) Hegelians, most notably J. B. Stallo.

Pragmatism

Charles Sanders Peirce, *Philosophical Writings of Peirce,* ed. Justus
Buchler; *The Essential Peirce: Selected Philosophical Writings,*
2 vols., ed. Peirce Edition Project; *Pragmatism as a Principle
and Method of Right Thinking: The 1903 Lectures on
Pragmatism,* ed. P. A. Turrisi.

William James, *Principles of Psychology,* 2 vols.; *The Varieties of
Religious Experience: A Study in Human Nature; Pragmatism,*
ed. B. Kuklick.

John Dewey, *Experience and Nature; The Quest for Certainty;
Logic: The Theory of Inquiry; Art as Experience; Human Nature
and Conduct; Theory of the Moral Life.*

George Herbert Mead, *Mind, Self, and Society.*

C. I. Lewis, *Mind and the World Order: Outline of a Theory of
Knowledge.*

Philosophical Analysis

Vienna Circle (1922–38): "logical positivism." Members were Hans Hahn, Philipp Frank, Otto Neurath, Moritz Schlick, Rudolf Carnap, Herbert Feigl, Friedrich Waismann, Gustav Bergmann, Viktor Kraft, and Bella von Juhos; associates included Kurt Gödel, Karl Menger, Felix Kaufmann, and Edgar Zilsel. A foundational figure was Ernst Mach, *The Science of Mechanics,* trans. T. J. McCormack.

Gottlob Frege, *The Foundations of Arithmetic: A Logico-Mathematical Enquiry into the Concept of Number,* trans. J. L. Austin; "Über Sinn und Bedeutung" is available in two translations: "On Sense and Nominatum," trans. H. Feigl in *Readings in Philosophical Analysis,* ed. H. Feigl and A. S. Sellars; and "On Sense and Reference," trans. M. Black in *Translations from the Philosophical Writings of Gottlob Frege,* ed. P. Geach and M. Black.

G. E. Moore, *Principia Ethica; Philosophical Studies;* "The Proof of an External World," in *Philosophical Papers.*

Bertrand Russell, "The Philosophy of Logical Atomism," *The Monist* 28 (1918); *Our Knowledge of the External World; An Inquiry into Meaning and Truth; Human Knowledge: Its Scope and Limits.*

Ludwig Wittgenstein, *Tractatus Logico-Philosophicus,* trans. D. F. Pears and B. F. McGuinness; *Philosophical Investigations,* 2nd ed., trans. G. E. M. Anscombe; *The Blue and Brown Books.*

Rudolf Carnap, *The Logical Structure of the World,* trans. R. George; *Logical Syntax of Language,* trans. A. Smeaton; "Testability and Meaning," *Philosophy of Science* 3 (1936): 419–71, and 4 (1937): 1–40.

A. J. Ayer, *Language, Truth and Logic* (the classic statement of logical positivism in English); *The Foundations of Empirical Knowledge.*

Gilbert Ryle, *The Concept of Mind; Dilemmas.*

Karl Popper, *The Logic of Scientific Discovery; Conjectures and Refutations; The Open Society and Its Enemies.*

J. L. Austin, *Sense and Sensibilia; How to Do Things with Words.*

Unity of Science Movement (1930s–1960s)

International group of philosophers and scientists; created the project of an *International Encyclopedia of Unified Science,* begun in 1938 and planned for twenty-six volumes, with the aim of developing a unified scientific language and eliciting the fundamental correlations between the various sciences. The result was a series of monographs by various authors published by the University of Chicago Press that ranged from John Dewey, *Theory of Valuation* (1939), to Thomas S. Kuhn, *The Structure of Scientific Revolutions* (1962). These were collected in two large volumes, *Foundations of the Unity of Science: Toward an International Encyclopedia of Unified Science,* ed. Otto Neurath, Rudolf Carnap, and Charles Morris (1971). Among other figures involved were Bertrand Russell, Ernst Nagel, Niels Bohr, Phillipp Frank, Carl G. Hempel, Herbert Feigl, Alfred Tarski, and L. Susan Stebbing.

Phenomenological and Existential Philosophy

Franz Brentano, *Psychology from an Empirical Standpoint,* trans. A. C. Rancurello, D. B. Terrell, and L. L. McAlister.

Alexius Meinong, "The Theory of Objects," in *Realism and the Background of Phenomenology,* ed. R. M. Chisholm.

Edmund Husserl, *Ideas,* vol. 1, trans. F. P. Kerston, vol. 2, trans. R. Rojcewicz and A. Schuwer, vol. 3, trans. T. E. Kline and W. E. Pohl; *Logical Investigations,* 2 vols., trans. J. N. Findlay; *The Crisis of European Sciences and Transcendental Phenomenology,* trans. D. Carr.

Martin Heidegger, *Being and Time*, trans. J. Macquarrie and
E. Robinson; see also the translation by J. Stambaugh; *An
Introduction to Metaphysics*, trans. R. Manheim. See also *Basic
Writings* (includes "The Origin of the Work of Art"), ed.
D. F. Krell.

Miguel de Unamuno, *The Tragic Sense of Life in Men and Nations*,
trans. A. Kerrigan.

Karl Jaspers, *Karl Jaspers: Basic Philosophical Writings, Selections*,
ed. and trans. L. H. Ehrlich, E. Ehrlich, and G. B. Pepper;
Man in the Modern Age, trans. E. Paul and C. Paul.

Jean-Paul Sartre, *Being and Nothingness: An Essay on
Phenomenological Ontology*, trans. H. E. Barnes; *The Psychology
of the Imagination*, trans. B. Frachtman.

Maurice Merleau-Ponty, *Phenomenology of Perception*, trans.
C. Smith; *The Visible and the Invisible*, trans. A. Lingis.

Neo-Kantianism

Turn-of-the-century movement that had its roots in Otto
Liebmann's motto "Back to Kant" in *Kant und die Epigonen*
(1865). Metaphysical (realistic) neo-Kantianism: Alois
Riehl; Marburg school: Hermann Cohen, Paul Natorp,
and early writings of Ernst Cassirer; neo-Friesian school,
Göttingen (based on Jakob Friedrich Fries's psychological
Kant-interpretation): Leonard Nelson; Heidelberg school
(also called Baden or southwest German school): Wilhem
Windelband and Heinrich Rickert; sociological neo-
Kantianism: Georg Simmel.

Idealistic and Speculative Philosophy

F. H. Bradley, *Appearance and Reality: A Metaphysical Essay;
Ethical Studies.*

Bernard Bosanquet, *The Principle of Individuality and Value* and *The Value and Destiny of the Individual* (the Gifford lectures for 1911 and 1912, respectively).

Josiah Royce, *The World and the Individual*, 2 vols.

Henri Bergson, *Creative Evolution*, trans. A. Mitchell; *Introduction to Metaphysics*, trans. T. E. Hulme; *The Two Sources of Morality and Religion*, trans. R. A. Audra and C. Brereton.

Samuel Alexander, *Space, Time, and Deity*.

Alfred North Whitehead, *Science and the Modern World; Process and Reality: An Essay in Cosmology; Adventures of Ideas*.

Kitarō Nishida, *An Inquiry into the Good*, trans. M. Abe and C. Ives. Japan's most distinguished philosopher of this period.

American Realist Movement

New realists: Ralph Barton Perry, William Pepperell Montague, Edwin Holt, Edwin Spaulding, Walter Marvin, and Walter Pitkin published "The Program and First Platform of Six Realists" in the *Journal of Philosophy* (1910) and authored a volume of essays, *The New Realism* (1912).

Critical realists: see *Essays in Critical Realism: A Cooperative Study of the Problem of Knowledge* (1920), containing position papers by Durant Drake, A. O. Lovejoy, J. P. Pratt, A. K. Rogers, C. A. Strong, George Santayana, and Roy Wood Sellars.

Philosophy of Religion

Rudolf Otto, *The Idea of the Holy: An Inquiry into the Non-Rational Factor in the Idea of the Divine and Its Relation to the Rational*, trans. J. W. Harvey.

Paul Tillich, *Systematic Theology*, 3 vols.; *The Courage To Be; Theology of Culture*, ed. R. C. Kimball.

Martin Buber, *I and Thou,* trans. R. G. Smith; *Between Man and Man,* trans. R. G. Smith.

Karl Barth, *The Word of God and the Word of Man,* trans. D. Horton; *The Humanity of God,* trans. J. N. Thomas.

Rudolf Bultmann, *Kerygma and Myth: A Theological Debate,* trans. R. H. Fuller; *History and Eschatology.*

Reinhold Niebuhr, *The Nature and Destiny of Man: A Christian Interpretation,* 2 vols.; *The Self and the Dramas of History.*

Dietrich Bonhoeffer, *Ethics,* trans. N. H. Smith; *Letters and Papers from Prison,* trans. R. H. Fuller and others.

Neo-Thomism

Étienne Gilson, *The Unity of Philosophical Experience; Being and Some Philosophers.*

Jacques Maritain, *The Degrees of Knowledge; Art and Scholasticism; Integral Humanism; A Preface to Metaphysics.*

Marxist Social and Political Philosophy

Vladimir Ilich Lenin, *Materialism and Empirio-Criticism: Critical Comments on a Reactionary Philosophy; State and Revolution.*

Frankfurt School: a movement founded at the Institute for Social Research, Frankfurt, in 1929 to develop a program for a "critical theory of society" through a continuance of the Marxist transformation of moral philosophy into social and political critique, with the goal of linking theory and practice. Permanent members included Max Horkheimer, Theodor W. Adorno, Herbert Marcuse, Erich Fromm, and Walter Benjamin.

Philosophical Anthropology

Wilhelm Dilthey, *The Formation of the Historical World in the Human Sciences*, vol. 3 of *Selected Works*, ed. R. A. Makkreel and F. Rodi.

Nicolai Hartmann, *Ethics*, 3 vols., trans. S. Coit.

Max Ferdinand Scheler, *Formalism in Ethics and Non-Formal Ethics of Values*, trans. M. S. Frings and R. Funk; *The Nature of Sympathy*, trans. P. Heath.

George Santayana, *The Life of Reason, or The Phases of Human Progress*, 5 vols.; *Scepticism and Animal Faith; The Sense of Beauty.*

Nicolai Berdyaev, *The Destiny of Man*, trans. N. Duddington; *The Beginning and the End*, trans. R. M. French; *The Meaning of History*, trans. G. Reavey.

Benedetto Croce, *Aesthetic as Science of Expression and General Linguistic*, trans. D. Ainslee; *Philosophy, Poetry, History: An Anthology of Essays*, trans. C. Sprigge.

R. G. Collingwood, *Speculum Mentis, or The Map of Knowledge; An Essay on Philosophical Method; Principles of Art; The Idea of History.*

José Ortega y Gassett, *The Revolt of the Masses*, trans. A. Kerrigan; *Man and People*, trans. W. R. Trask; *Meditations on Quixote*, trans. E. Rugg and D. Marin.

Ernst Cassirer, *The Philosophy of Symbolic Forms*, vols. 1–3, trans. R. Manheim, vol. 4, trans. J. M. Krois, ed. J. M. Krois and D. P. Verene; *An Essay on Man: An Introduction to a Philosophy of Human Culture; The Myth of the State; Symbol, Myth, and Culture: Essays and Lectures of Ernst Cassirer 1935–1945*, ed. D. P. Verene.

Commentaries: Twentieth Century

A. J. Ayer, ed., *Logical Positivism.*

I. Benrubi, *Contemporary Thought in France.*

I. M. Bochenski, *Contemporary European Philosophy.*

J. Collins, *The Existentialists.*

F. Copleston, *Contemporary Philosophy.*

L. D. Easton, *Hegel's First American Followers: The Ohio Hegelians.*

H. Feigl and W. Sellars, eds., *Readings in Philosophical Analysis.*

R. L. Hawkins, *Positivism in the United States.*

M. Jay, *The Dialectical Imagination: A History of the Frankfurt School and the Institute for Social Research 1923–1950.*

V. Kraft, *The Vienna Circle.*

A. W. Levi, *Philosophy and the Modern World.*

J. Passmore, *A Hundred Years of Philosophy.*

H. A. Pochmann, *New England Transcendentalism and St. Louis Hegelianism: Phases in the History of American Idealism.*

A. J. Reck, *Recent American Philosophy.*

H. Reichenbach, *The Rise of Scientific Philosophy.*

H. W. Schneider, *A History of American Philosophy.*

H. Spiegelberg, *The Phenomenological Movement,* 2 vols.

J. O. Urmson, *Philosophical Analysis: Its Development Between the Two World Wars.*

J. Wahl, *A Short History of Existentialism.*

G. J. Warnock, *English Philosophy Since 1900.*

M. Warnock, *Ethics Since 1900.*

W. H. Werkmeister, *A History of Philosophical Ideas in America.*

General Histories of Philosophy and Works of General Interest

E. T. Bell, *The Development of Mathematics.*

G. Boas, *The Major Traditions of European Philosophy.*

B. Bosanquet, *A History of Aesthetic.*

E. T. H. Brann, *The World of the Imagination: Sum and Substance.*

E. Bréhier, *History of Philosophy,* 7 vols.

C. D. Broad, *Five Types of Ethical Theory.*

G. E. Cairns, *Philosophies of History: Meeting of East and West in Cycle-Pattern Theories of History.*

F. Cajori, *A History of Mathematics.*

J. Collins, *A History of Modern European Philosophy.*

————, *Interpreting Modern Philosophy.*

F. Copleston, *A History of Philosophy,* 9 vols.

W. R. Crawford, *A Century of Latin-American Thought.*

T. J. De Boer, *The History of Philosophy in Islam.*

C. J. Ducasse, *Philosophy as a Science.*

J. M. Edie and others, eds., *Russian Philosophy,* 3 vols.

J. E. Erdmann, *A History of Philosophy,* 2 vols.

É. Gilson, *History of Philosophy and Philosophical Education.*

J. J. E. Gracia, *Philosophy and Its History: Issues in Philosophical Historiography.*

J. J. E. Gracia, M. Reichberg, and B. N. Schumacher, eds., *The Classics of Western Philosophy: A Reader's Guide.*

E. Grassi, *Philosophy and Rhetoric: The Humanist Tradition.*

G. W. F. Hegel, *Lectures on the History of Philosophy,* 3 vols., trans. E. S. Haldane and F. H. Simson.

H. Höffding, *A History of Modern Philosophy,* 2 vols.

K. Jaspers, *The Great Philosophers.*

W. Kneale and M. Kneale, *The Development of Logic.*

F. A. Lange, *The History of Materialism and Criticism of Its Present Importance.*

S. Langer, *Philosophy in a New Key.*

A. W. Levi, *Philosophy as Social Expression.*

A. O. Lovejoy, *The Great Chain of Being.*

B. Mazlish, *The Riddle of History: The Great Speculators from Vico to Freud.*

G. H. R. Parkinson and S. G. Shanker, eds., *Routledge History of Philosophy,* 10 vols.

J. H. Randall, *The Career of Philosophy.*

H. Sidgwick, *Outline of the History of Ethics.*

C. Singer, *A Short History of Science.*

H. R. Smart, *Philosophy and Its History.*

W. T. Stace, *Mysticism and Philosophy.*

L. Thorndike, *A History of Magic and Experimental Science,* 8 vols.

F. Ueberweg, *History of Philosophy,* 2 vols.

E. Underhill, *Mysticism.*

B. Vickers, *In Defence of Rhetoric.*

E. Westermarck, *The Origin and Development of Moral Ideas,* 2 vols.

B. Williams, *The Sense of the Past: Essays in the History of Philosophy.*

W. Windelband, *A History of Philosophy,* 2 vols.

Philosophical Perspectives

ON READING PHILOSOPHICAL BOOKS

The classics are the books that come down to us bearing the traces
of readings previous to ours, and bringing in their wake the traces
they themselves have left on culture or cultures they have passed
through.

—Italo Calvino, *The Uses of Literature*

Ars Critica and *Ars Topica*

Philosophical books require the reader to pass dialectically between
two poles as they are read: a critical pole, by which the reader seeks
to form a judgment of the work, and a topical pole, by which the
reader seeks to enter the work and appreciate it for what it is.
These two poles match the general distinction within thought
defined by the ancients and taken up by the Renaissance humanists as the *ars critica* and *ars topica,* a distinction that has been all
but lost in the development of modern philosophy.

The fourth part of the *Port-Royal Logic* or *L'Art de Penser* of
Antoine Arnauld and Pierre Nicole, published in 1662, makes
a distinction between two methods of thinking: analysis and

synthesis. Analysis is the method for discovering truth and is called *method of resolution* or *invention.* Synthesis is the method for making truth understandable once it is found and is called *method of composition* or *doctrine.*[1] This formulation of method is an extraordinary development in the history of the modern theory of knowledge. It reconceives the classical humanist conception of *inventio,* making it part of the *ars critica* by removing it from the *ars topica. Inventio,* or the amassing of materials necessary to the beginning of any inquiry, now becomes part of critical method.

The art of topics, or the art of finding the starting points for the most probable lines of reasoning on a subject, the mastery of which Cicero claimed was the basis of his eloquence, is excluded from the process of rational thought. Arnauld and Nicole never directly attack the *ars topica* of classical rhetoric; they simply place it outside method and do not acknowledge any rhetorical basis for logic. In their view, invention is not the drawing forth of a plausible starting point from the stance of common wisdom. It is instead the resolving into proper arrangement of the parts relevant to a particular inquiry. The *ars topica* is thus absorbed into the *ars critica.* In its classical conception, rhetoric, in addition to its command of the *ars topica,* is also necessary as the means to persuade an audience of a truth. In the *Port-Royal Logic,* the method of synthesis replaces persuasion with *demonstratio.* The method of synthesis composes the results of the inquiry, so their truth is proved doctrine. There is no need for persuasion, because when properly proved a truth needs no further statement. Invention and its demonstration now appear to be open to everyone who possesses the Cartesian *bon sens.*

In the *Port-Royal Logic,* Descartes' method of the *Discourse* is turned into a theory of education. The traditional rhetorical basis of logic disappears; all thinking becomes the application of critical method to whatever appears before the mind. Gone is Aristotle's twofold theory of the syllogism: the syllogism as an instrument of demonstration and the syllogism as a means for the generation of ideas.[2] The methods for testing the validity of syllogisms presuppose the presence of a syllogism to test. The question remains as to how the syllogism is generated in the first place. The generation of a syllogism requires the art of topics or the art of the middle term, which is the medium that connects the major and minor terms of a syllogism. The middle term is present only in the premises and disappears in the conclusion. This middle term that makes the syllogism come into being requires a meaning that is held in common between the speaker's intention and the listeners; it is, namely, a commonplace. From such a common ground derived from a practice of the art of topics, the speaker can draw forth the connection of the terms of the conclusion, and the syllogism can be tested by the *ars critica* or logic.

Lost in the education in method is the mentality of topics—the focus on how something is generated. Critique, critical thinking, the evaluation of arguments and evidence become the dominant occupation of thought. This new non-rhetorical conception of thinking that stems from Descartes and the *Port-Royal Logic,* joined with the sense of criticism and *raisonnement* of the Enlightenment, shapes our approach to reading philosophical books. We are all critics. Our immediate instinct is to check and test what is said in a philosophical text as we go through it. Attention to the question of the truth of what is said takes precedence over, or at least directs, the question of its meaning. There is an unconscious presumption by the reader that what is meant is already known; the problem is to assess it.

Fascination with method is fascination with critique, for method is always the idea of a standard that can separate truth from error, and this standard in the end is logic in the Port-Royal sense of analysis and synthesis or later variants thereof. So much attention is given by the typical philosophical reader to the argumentative and evidential aspects of what is said that little awareness is achieved of how it is said or from where its ideas are generated. In other words, philosophical books are logically but not at the same time rhetorically grasped. Their rhetorical features are as irrelevant to the thought that they contain as rhetoric is to the Cartesian project of the establishment of the method of right reasoning. In this way, the great works in the history of philosophy as well as contemporary works of philosophical thought are not read as a whole; they are not comprehended as literature of a particular type. They are not comprehended as literature at all. They are approached as pure productions of the mind; all else that may be present is incidental to evaluating the truth or falsity that may lie therein.

This portrait of the modern philosophical reader is deliberately put in somewhat strong relief. Certainly the style and manner of texts affect and draw the reader to them, but it is how these features of the texts are regarded that make a difference in the reader's comprehension of the texts. We must recover the mentality of the art of finding the starting points of thought, the *ars topica,* in order to apply successfully to such texts the principles of criticism, the *ars critica.* If I say to a child, "Go into the garden and see if there is any pachysandra there," the child asks: "What is pachysandra?" It is as simple as that—questions of meaning precede questions of truth.

We cannot argue about the truth of Plato's doctrine of form (*eidos*) unless we begin by understanding the development of *eidos* in Greek literature, that its first meaning and usage in Homer is "what one sees," "appearance" or "shape," normally of the body, a sense that was continued in pre-Socratic philosophy. By the time of Herodotus, *eidos* and its cognate *idea* had been extended into "characteristic property" or "type." It also became a technical medical term linked to *dynamis,* meaning something like "constitutive nature" as employed by Hippocrates.

All words have histories as well as multiple meanings. Until the crucial words of a philosophical doctrine are understood in terms of the history of their meanings and the sense in which they are employed by the particular philosophical book being read, no viable critical evaluation is possible. In *Process and Reality* A. N. Whitehead said that "it is more important that a proposition be interesting than that it be true. The importance of truth is, that it adds to interest."[3] Interest must first be directed to finding the meaning of these key terms of a philosophy. These meanings are tied not only to the word's etymology but to the period of thought in which the work was written and to the aims of its author. To approach the comprehension of a work in critical terms is to remain external to it, to fail to penetrate its inner form. To discover a work's inner form, philosophy must be joined with philology. We must be willing to enter into the sense of the author's language and the author's world and to attempt to find in them the questions the author is asking. This requires not only intellectual empathy but also the objective formulation of what the question is that the author is pursuing.

Argument and Narration

The propensity to embed philosophy in the *ars critica* has produced the view that the essence of philosophy is argument. That philosophy depends on argument is taken as such common knowledge that to dispute it seems simply to abandon philosophy for some other form of thinking. But when we speak of philosophical argument we cannot conceive of it simply as logical argument following the rules of formal reasoning. Philosophical arguments are couched in rhetorical forms of speech that make them understandable to the hearer or reader and that account for a great part of their acceptability and usefulness. This is not to say that philosophical argument can be solely rhetorical in nature, depending only on techniques of speech and language for its success.

Is philosophy about arguments? Is argument, whatever we may wish to understand by it, at the heart of philosophy? Does the truth of any philosophy rest on its arguments? Or do the arguments we identify within a total philosophy or within a philosophical position depend upon a form of thinking and speech that is itself not argumentative?

Ernesto Grassi, working from the insights and texts of the Italian humanist tradition from the Renaissance to Vico, has suggested that all rationalistic speech—speech having arguments and deductions as its basic form—depends upon another form of speech that is non-rationalistic, non-argumentative, and non-deductive.[4] This is the speech of first principles, or *archai*. Grassi observes that the starting points of any deductive reasoning are not supplied by the deduction itself. It is a scandal to logic that it cannot ground its own starting points. For this a speech that follows tropic, not logical, patterns is necessary, especially the metaphor. Grassi sees this as the fundamental moment at which logic or argument requires rhetoric. Rhetorical speech grounds the beginning points of reasoning itself.

Rhetoric is not tied to philosophical reasoning as a way to make its conclusions more understandable and communicative, or to provide a way to state more loosely what can in principle be put into the formal terms of logical thought. Instead, rhetoric is required in order that logic or argument in philosophy can exist at all. The metaphor is the basis of philosophical thought, and the act of imagination that the discovery of the metaphor requires is at the heart of the philosophical enterprise. The argument makes clear in rationalistic terms what the mind has a primordial access to in the metaphor and in the rhetorically organized speech of first principles. This approach makes rhetoric a necessary moment in argument. It identifies rhetoric in philosophical reasoning with the speech act in which the argument is initiated. The art of rhetoric is the art of first principles, the art of finding the topics from which a line of reasoning can be generated. This conception of the art of rhetoric accomplishes the ancient connection between topics and probable reasoning. The topos is that from which we "draw forth" what is needed for probable reasoning.

I would like to add to Grassi's view some observations about philosophical systems which I think are compatible with it and help illuminate the role of argument in such systems. We must consider philosophical arguments not just in isolation, but in relation to total or full-blown philosophies. If Grassi is correct, the speech act wherein *archai* are adduced is essentially narrative. The narrative act exists in the way the metaphor begins the speech of the argument. The narrative also holds the individual arguments of a total philosophy together. By "total philosophies" I mean most of those espoused by the major figures studied in the history of Western philosophy. A philosophy is not simply a collection of arguments put together in one place.

What holds a philosophy together is its narrative aspect. The narrative it expresses is the life blood that animates its arguments and gives them interest. Arguments are not interesting in themselves; they are interesting only for the role they play in some expressed or implied narrative. If an argument is examined by itself, it is ultimately interesting only when it is brought back into some narrative of which it is a part. Philosophers in the Anglo-American analytic tradition often claim that certain arguments are just interesting in themselves, but even in such cases there actually is a narrative in which these arguments that are "just interesting" exist. This narrative may be no more than the articulation that could be done of the analytic Weltanschauung itself or some more specific part of it as applied to the self, the mind, ethics, or things.

Every philosophy is an attempt to think through a question to an answer. For total philosophies, or philosophies of the whole, the question is without limits. Arguments must be mediated within some context that is not itself argued, but that is simply there. The form of this context, what holds the specific arguments together, or makes them interesting, is the narrative dimension of philosophy. The natural form of the meditation is the narration.

Image and Question

What are the commonplaces from which the author produces the narrative that is the author's philosophy? How is the reader to proceed in this matter? Where is the reader to find these topoi that the reader may share with the author? These topics or commonplaces lie within or depend upon the images present in philosophical works. These images are not simply adornments of the author's thought, to be passed by as inessential to the work. They are the keys to the starting points and to the continuing perspective of the work. Philosophical books are works not only of the intellect but also of the imagination. In *The Philosophical Imaginary,* the French philosopher Michèle Le Doeuff says:

> Whether one looks for a characterization of philosophical discourse to Plato, to Hegel or to Bréhier, one always meets with a reference to the rational, the concept, the argued, the logical, the abstract. Even when a certain coyness leads some authorities to pretend that they do not know what philosophy is, no agnosticism remains about what philosophy is not. Philosophy is not a story, not a pictorial description, not a work of pure literature. Philosophical discourse is inscribed and declares its status as philosophy through a break with myth, fable, the poetic, the domain of the image.

Le Doeuff claims further:

> If, however, one goes looking for this philosophy in the texts which are meant to embody it, the least that can be said is that it is not to be found there in a pure state. We shall *also* find statues that breathe the scent of roses, comedies, tragedies, architects, foundations, dwellings, doors and windows, sand, navigators, various musical instruments, islands, clocks, horses, donkeys and even a lion, representatives of every craft and trade, scenes of sea and storm, forests and trees: in short, a whole pictorial world sufficient to decorate even the dryest "History of Philosophy."[5]

La Doeuff is surely right. We keep philosophy in mind through its metaphors: Heraclitus's river, Plato's cave, Aristotle's sea battle, Augustine's pear tree, Anselm's fool, Ockham's razor, Machiavelli's prince, Bacon's idols, Descartes' *poêle,* Spinoza's bondage, Leibniz's windowless monads, Pascal's wager, Locke's candle, Berkeley's tar water, Hume's fork, Kant's fog banks of illusion, Mill's canons, Hegel's master and servant, Marx's fetish, Smith's hidden hand, Russell's logical atom, Wittgenstein's family resemblance, Husserl's bracketing, Heidegger's *Holzweg*, Quine's bound variable. There is no end to the lists and sublists for the history of philosophy or lists for individual philosophies that could be constructed. The history of philosophy in terms of the images and master images employed by major philosophers has yet to be written. But it is written in our heads. It is through the images and in terms of the images that we in fact do recall and have access to philosophies and to the whole history of philosophy. Are such images accidental to its nature, to its use of language, or are they a necessary component of philosophical truth and its statement? My answer is that the metaphor or image is not only typical of philosophical expression, it is a necessary part of it.

Rhetoric and poetic join each other in the metaphorical image. The metaphor is what gives thought life and what transfers to the reader the liveliness of the thought of the work. In *Ars Poetica* Horace says the purpose of poetry is to instruct, delight, and move (333). Cicero attributes the same three qualities to rhetoric (*Brutus*, 276). For the critical, as opposed to the speculative, thinker, philosophical books seem only to instruct; they seem to be only discursive prose documents stating claims and arguments to be examined, as discussed in chapter 1. R. G. Collingwood in *An Essay on Philosophical Method* says that philosophical literature is chiefly prose, but prose punctuated with poetic insight. He says that "the philosopher must go to school with the poets in order to learn the use of language."[6] Collingwood's assertion echoes Hegel's comment in the fragment on "The Earliest System-Program of German Idealism" that "poetry is the teacher of humanity."[7] For the great philosopher, the poetic image is never far from the logically formed thought.

It is in its images that a philosophical text tends to delight and, to an extent, to move. Once one begins to give attention to the presence of images in philosophical works, they appear much more numerous and more insightful than is usually thought, especially in regard to the modern model of critical reading. Umberto Eco says that when dealing with written texts, we "must presuppose a literal degree zero from which metaphor is the departure that must be interpreted." He says: "It is also true that if we look at things from the glottogonic point of view (whether at the origins of language, as Vico wanted, or at the origins of every text that comes into being), we must take account of the moment when creativity can emerge, for it does so only at the cost of a metaphorical vagueness that names an object that is yet unknown or unnamed."[8] This view that Eco advances of literature generally, applies specifically to philosophical texts.

The philosopher does not claim to say all that literally can be said, but neither does the philosopher aim at a speech that is complete only in principle. The speech of the whole must itself be a whole; that is, it must speak of the little and big, the near and far, the particular and general, the familiar and the unfamiliar, the ordinary and the extraordinary. Of such a procedure we should be able to say what Vico reminds us was said of Demosthenes, who came forth from the Platonic Academy "armed with his invincible enthymeme, which he formed by means of a very well regulated excess, going outside his case into quite distant things with which he tempered the lightning flashes of his arguments, which, when striking, amazed the listeners so much the more by how much he had diverted them."[9] The most vital part of a philosophical discourse is to be found in the digression. The reader should never fail to examine closely a digression or digressive statement.

In a time when rhetoric is lacking from most modern education and thought, we must remember that eloquence refers to the completeness of a speech, not the elegance or ornament of the phraseology. To be a good speaker, to speak with eloquence, the speaker must say all there is to say, appropriately, about a subject, to take the audience through all the aspects that can be drawn out of the subject matter. To draw all of this forth in language

that offers both the details of the subject and its generalities is
to speak with eloquence. Such a speech will naturally bear the
mark of wisdom. Eloquence and wisdom (*eloquentia* and *sapientia*)
go hand in hand: true philosophy is wisdom speaking. Quintilian
reminds us that Cicero (*De Oratore,* 14.63–64) holds that invention (*inventio*) and arrangement (*dispositio*) are in the range of
anyone, but that eloquence is another matter. I take Cicero's point
to be that anyone can in fact think, either because of the presence
of natural powers of intelligence and talent for a subject matter
or because of this talent coupled with proper training. But the
production of thought into language is a matter of special importance and does not follow unproblematically from the power of
natural or trained thought. This does not deny that the ancients
allowed for the possibility of natural eloquence in a speaker, for
they did.

Cicero thought eloquence of special importance, and Quintilian
says, that Cicero was "justified in so doing is shown clearly by the
actual name of the art of which I am speaking. For the verb *eloqui*
means the production and communication to the audience of all
that the speaker has conceived in his mind" (*Institutio Oratoria,*
8.15–16). The partial mind in philosophy makes the partial
speech, ineloquent and ultimately useless, no matter how high-
sounding and how nicely such partial speech may turn phrases
and arguments and even please with ornament and elegance. To
have done and organized the research, which is what the stages
of *inventio* and *dispositio* mean, in modern terms, and then to be
unable to re-create the total in language of what is in the mind, to
use Quintilian's words, "is as useless as a sword that is kept permanently within its sheath" (ibid.).

Philosophy cannot avoid rhetoric, but it cannot avoid poetry,
either. It cannot avoid poetry because it cannot avoid tropes. For
philosophy to engage in the eloquent speech of the whole and thus
to aim at the production of the true in language—to make the true
appear to the philosopher and his audience in words—requires
topics (topoi), those loci or general commonplaces upon which the

philosopher must depend in order to make his speech. Topoi have been called by Vico the "art of the middle term." Aristotle in the *Prior Analytics* (70b1–5) describes how from the grasp of a middle term the other terms of the syllogism can be constructed from an enthymeme and an argument correctly formed, as mentioned earlier. Topics are a vast subject about which both the ancients and the moderns have written, but however topics as a subject are to be understood, it is clear that philosophers, like everyone else who wishes to speak fully and understandably on a subject, must draw forth what is said from some basic mental places. In some way these must command some "common" intelligibility in a fashion analogous to the need for the middle term as that which must be found in order to make a desired connection between the other two terms of a syllogism.

The thought of anything new is always poetic. The metaphor makes a new connection between elements of experience. Aristotle says: "But the greatest thing by far is to be a master of metaphor. It is the one thing that cannot be learnt from others; and it is also a sign of genius, since a good metaphor implies an intuitive perception of the similarity in dissimilars" (*Poetics* 1459a 5–8). This, we may say, is as true for the philosopher as for the poet.

How, then, in terms of what has already been said here, can philosophy be differentiated from poetry? In discussions of the poetic nature of philosophic thought, this is always the final question. It never fails to be asked. It is as if the philosopher, having believed from the first study of philosophy forward that philosophy was a project of reason and argument, of concept formation and discursive truth, now sees philosophy disappearing into the well of poetry, the concept passing out of existence into the image, the argument being laid out for burial, to be interred within the story, the narrative, the lyric, or the fable. The forms of reason are just transparencies of thought about to disappear into the richness and immediacy of the speech of the poet. Would it not be better to maintain the myth of the rationality of philosophy, shameful as it may be, rather than risk the loss of philosophy itself into the language of the image and the passions? Has acknowledgment of the poetic element in reason come too far to return to assert the traditional conceptual and logical purposes of philosophical thought?

What prevents philosophy from becoming poetry is not the fact that philosophy can take discursive form. Other forms of thought can occur in discursive language: science or history, for example. What keeps philosophy from becoming a story or a series of metaphorical understandings is the presence of the question. It is no accident that philosophy, at least in the sense of self-knowledge, originated in the Socratic discovery of the question. Cicero says, "Socrates was the first to call philosophy down from the heavens and set her in the cities of men and bring her also into their homes and compel her to ask questions about life and morality and things good and evil" (*Tusculan Disputations*, 5.4.10). Socrates did this by attaching philosophy to the device of the question. The ability to ask questions is distinctive to human beings, to the one animal that takes its own existence as a problem and that is capable of both wonder and laughter.

It is the question that takes us beyond the image, and the continual presence of the question keeps philosophical thought from receding back into the poem, into the images upon which it depends for its formulation and communication. The image or metaphor, the story or fable always *presents*. As Susanne Langer states it: "Metaphor is our most striking evidence of *abstractive seeing*, of the power of human minds to use presentational symbols. Every new experience, or new idea about things, evokes first of all some metaphorical expression."[10]

Metaphors provide thought with the immediate sense of reality and the new connection that provides for beginnings. The image is always a moment of *archē*. True beginning points in speech require the connection of the metaphor, as Aristotle suggests. The question, however, establishes motion. It is inherently dialectical. It does not hold things together so much as it pushes them apart and throws them into opposition. The metaphor coming suddenly into mind gives thought a new place to be. The question makes the metaphor into a thought. What the metaphorical image establishes, the question throws into intellectual relief.

Examples from Modern Philosophy: Descartes, Hobbes, Kant, Hegel

Descartes, at the beginning of the "Second Meditation," draws an analogy between himself and Archimedes to emphasize that he will continue his project of hypothetical doubt until either he recognizes something as certain or establishes for certain that there is no certainty. He says: "Archimedes used to demand just one firm and immovable point in order to shift the entire earth; so I too can hope for great things if I manage to find just one thing, however slight, that is certain and unshakeable."[11] Descartes may be thinking of Plutarch's comment on Archimedes in his life of Marcellus that "Archimedes, who was a kinsman and friend of King Hiero, wrote to him that with any given force it was possible to move any given weight; and emboldened, as we are told, by the strength of his demonstration, he declared that, if there were another world, and he could go to it, he could move this."[12] Archimedes' demonstration for King Hiero was to move a three-masted merchant ship that had been dragged ashore by a great labor of many men, by quietly setting in motion by his own hand a system of triple pulleys such that the ship moved toward him with ease.

The reader might at first glance think that Descartes has in mind the common version of Archimedes' claim that if he had a lever long enough and a place to stand, he could lift the earth. But the reader cannot presume this simply because it may likely be the version the reader has heard. Despite Descartes' denial of the pursuit of letters as a pathway to truth, he is a philosopher schooled in rhetoric and the classics. Descartes' analogy points to the principle of placing himself in another world in order to move this one. A pulley, like a divine force, moves by attraction. It is more subtle than the direct pressure of a lever that operates as an extension of the thing to which it is applied.

In the dedicatory letter to the dean and the Faculty of Theology of the Sorbonne that precedes the *Meditations*, Descartes says he has always thought that the two topics of God and the soul are subjects that ought to be given demonstrative proof with the aid of philosophy rather than theology.[13] He then says that we must believe in God because it is doctrine of Holy Scripture and that we must believe Holy Scripture because it comes from God.

Descartes says that both he and the doctors of the Faculty of Theology know this argument is true, but it cannot be successfully presented to unbelievers because they would judge it to be circular. In fact, it is a classic example of circular argument. Descartes proposes to leave the world of theology and enter the world of philosophy, which he now declares to be outside the former. From this world of philosophy he can accomplish his Archimedean task. In a single, ironic stroke Descartes inverts the principle of all Scholastic thought: that philosophy is the servant of theology. The world of philosophical reason is now a place outside theology's circle of faith that completes reason, and Descartes with his Archimedean pulley attracts us to this newly freed world. Descartes' triple-pulley device is his principle whereby he can prove with certainty the existence of the I, God, and finally the world. His guiding question has been: how can reason extricate itself from faith upon which theology depends at every turn?

Descartes' works abound with metaphors and topics taken from humanist thought: from the picture of himself as thinker in the *poêle*, the stove-heated room, of the *Discourse on Method* to reading the book of nature, to stepping upon the stage of the theater of the world, to his philosophical optics of the light of nature. His questions are always posed through his use of such tropes. Plato, having dismissed or seeming to have dismissed poetry in his dialogues, nevertheless stands as the most poetic of philosophers. Descartes, having dismissed rhetoric early in the *Discourse*, stands as one of the most richly rhetorical philosophers, constantly using images and tropes to draw his readers in.

Hobbes titles his most famous book *Leviathan*, taking the term from the biblical book of Job and using the term for the first time as a concept in secular literature. In his frontispiece Hobbes quotes from the Vulgate: "Upon the earth there is not his like." The second line that completes the verse is "a creature without fear" (Job 41:33). To approach *Leviathan* through a critical analysis of the claims of Hobbes's political philosophy is to miss much of the book as Hobbes conceived it. The book, from its title forward, is built on an analogy: as nature stands to ancient man, the state stands to modern man. God asks: "Can you draw out Leviathan with a fishhook, or press down his tongue with a cord?" (41:1). And God concludes: "It surveys everything that is lofty; it is king over all that are proud" (41:34). Leviathan is king over all proud creatures. The Lord calls attention to Leviathan to demonstrate the power of nature in relation to man. Job is the book of prudence for ancient man, who has no power to modify nature or to nego- tiate his condition with the Lord.

Hobbes's *Leviathan* is the book of Job for modern man. Modern man, through the development of the new science of nature, has begun to enact Bacon's claim that nature must be obeyed in order that it be commanded. Modern man does not live in direct contact with the Lord. The church is an intermediary, and the common- wealth of the Christian church stands in problematic relation to the commonwealth of the state. The state now stands to modern man as a power that "surveys everything that is lofty; it is king over all that are proud." Hobbes says: "The multitude so united in one Person, is called a COMMON-WEALTH, in latine CIVITAS. This is the Generation of the great LEVIATHAN, or rather (to speake more reverently) of that *Mortall God*, to which wee owe under the *Immortall God*, our peace and defense."[14] The *Leviathan*, as the book of Job for modern man, is an instruction as to how, having significant power over nature, modern man is to live within the absolute power of the monarch.

Arguments make sense only as they exist within some narrative. Arguments never simply stand on their own. They may seem to do so only if one is shortsighted enough not to see the larger tale which, either explicitly or implicitly, they presuppose and require. The arguments that make up Hobbes's political philosophy as they are critically examined presuppose his larger question: what is the human condition, once our relation to God and nature have assumed modern form—when the state is not simply the individual soul written in larger letters, but the individual writ large as the artificial man?

The key to Hobbes's *Leviathan* is to be found not only in its title but in the biblical analysis in its third and fourth books, in which he aims to show that his politics fits with what is said in Scripture. A crucial point is Hobbes's conception of the existence of "the kingdom of darkness," which rests largely upon the verse in Paul's Letter to the Ephesians that reads: "For our struggle is not against enemies of blood and flesh, but against the rulers, against the authorities, against the cosmic powers of this present darkness, against the spiritual forces of evil in the heavenly places" (6:12).

Hobbes's claim is that there is a spiritual darkness that threatens the proper understanding of the state and man and is based on a misinterpretation of Scripture that he wishes to correct.[15] Hobbes's call, in *Leviathan,* is for a new covenant (a call that in itself has a long biblical tradition behind it). Hobbes's use of the term *covenant* (which he distinguishes from *contract*) for his principle that lies at the basis of political life is meant to carry a biblical image. It is not simply intended as a logical idea. The new covenant derives from the proper comprehension of the divine wisdom of Scripture. Most commentators pass quickly over the third and fourth books of *Leviathan* or ignore them. Whether Hobbes is wholly sincere or not in his biblical exposition is a question to be considered, but it is clear that the topics, the commonplaces, from which Hobbes constructs his philosophy are pervasively biblical, and to pass by them is to lose the sense of his way of thinking and to lose the ground he intends to share with his reader. Hobbes even says one of his fears is his own power of rhetoric.

In the one poetic passage in the *Critique of Pure Reason*, Kant provides the reader with the key to his conception of the pure understanding. He has considered the whole territory of the pure understanding and assigned everything to its rightful place. He says:

> This domain [the pure understanding] is an island, enclosed by nature itself within unalterable limits. It is the land of truth—enchanting name!—surrounded by a wide and stormy ocean, the native home of illusion, where many a fog bank and many a swiftly melting iceberg give the deceptive appearance of farther shores, deluding the adventurous seafarer ever anew with empty hopes, and engaging him in enterprises which he never can abandon and yet is unable to carry to completion.[16]

Kant's "land of truth" where only the pure understanding reigns is the much-sought philosophical Eden, the isle of the blessed, the kingdom of Prester John, the self-contained world of Robinson Crusoe. It is the vision of a land of certainty, without error or ambiguity of any kind, a perfect, clean, and well-lighted dwelling place of the intellect.

Kant's image, like all such master images, comes into his text for the reader as news from nowhere. As the reader thinks it through, he grasps the sense of the central question that underlies Kant's transcendental method: how something is possible. Kant's concern is how something that is rationally possible apart from experience can at the same time be actual within experience. It is the question of "synthetic a posteriority." If Kant can separate understanding from reason, he can reach the blessed isle of true knowing that resists the propensity of reason to think beyond the determinate use of categories within experience to the possibilities of being itself, wherein lie the fog banks of illusion. By explicitly giving the reader both the question that dominates his intellect—how is such and such possible?—and the image of the blessed isle that dominates his imagination, Kant has given the reader access to the inner form of his philosophy.

Kant is also capable of giving the reader briefer yet just as profound metaphors. In the section on "Schematism" regarding the crucial principle of the union of sense-intuition and concept, Kant suddenly says that the schematism is "an art concealed in the depths of the human soul."[17] What kind of art is this? It is the art of having experience, of epistemological savoir faire. Those that inhabit the blessed isle of the pure understanding are the practitioners of this fundamental art. They are those who can assign everything its rightful place—the true critical philosophers, the philosophers of the pure understanding.

Hegel in the *Phenomenology of Spirit* calls the course consciousness takes in its self-development a "highway of despair" (*Weg der Verzweiflung*).[18] As consciousness passes from one stage to another, it slowly realizes it moves from one illusion to the next and that these illusions are somehow of its own making. Its sense of *aufheben*—of both preserving the previous stage in memory and yet at the same time canceling it as illusion—contains the danger of self-forgetting. Consciousness is constantly at risk of forgetting what it has experienced and thinking that it has finally arrived at a stage of absolute knowing. Hegel's highway of despair is the journey into the underworld that must be taken to attain what is needed for a grasp of the future, taken in order to master time and achieve the absolute.

Hegel's journey is the visit to the edge of the kingdom of the dead taken by Odysseus in the eleventh book of the *Odyssey*. It is the descent to the underworld by Aeneas, in the sixth book of the *Aeneid*, who from the Sibyl learns that he must secure a golden bough in order to pass safely through the region of the underworld and emerge from it. Having secured the golden bough and descended into the underworld, he learns from Anchises how he will marry Lavinia, and that from this union the Trojans will produce the race that will populate Latium and Italy. It is Dante who, in the first canto of the *Divine Comedy*, finds himself in a dark wood of error, having glimpsed the divine light of the *dilettoso monte*, the delectable mountain, with his way blocked by the three beasts—the she-wolf, leopard, and lion—which foreshadow the regions of the inferno that he must now traverse in order to reach his goal: to visit paradise. The golden bough that consciousness requires to attain to absolute knowing is Hegel's dialectic: the power to pass from being-in-itself to being-for-itself and then to commence the passage again, done from the new perspective gained in the previous movement, and the power not to forget the stages of the journey as it is accomplished.

The question hidden in Hegel's metaphor of the journey of consciousness is whether reason can be grasped as a process of self-determination, as emerging from the very nature of experience rather than finding its beginning points in a *Jenseits*, a beyond of experience. Hegel's *Phenomenology* is full of images, many of which organize whole stages of the work: the inverted world, the master and servant, the unhappy consciousness, the phrenological skull, the spiritual zoo, the beautiful soul, and so on. What underlies Hegel's golden bough of the dialectic is stated as a metaphor in the *Science of Logic*, where Hegel distinguishes between "bad infinity" and "true infinity." Bad infinity is the static dialectic of finitude and infinitude as simple opposites, as found in his stage of unhappy consciousness in the *Phenomenology*, in which infinitude is not truly unlimited, since it is infinitude only to the extent that it acts against finitude as an opposite limit. True infinity is the self-determinate process of a finite-in-an-infinite recapitulating itself in unending fashion, a sense of self-limiting infinity like that found on a bottle with a label that pictures a bottle with a label on it, and so on. Reason is always going beyond the being of a particular state, reaching out to the *dilettoso monte* of the absolute, which is ever within and without its grasp.

With these four examples of Descartes, Hobbes, Kant, and Hegel, I intend to suggest that in the great works in the history of philosophy there is a dialectic between the image and the question.

In them philosophy does not overcome but instead embodies that original interplay in the Platonic dialogues between the telling of a likely story or myth and the elenchus, the question-and-answer exchange of which Socrates is a master. In the dialogues this discursive exchange of the elenchus leads to the recasting of the subject under discussion in mythic narrative, which in turn leads back to the argument in the way that the *ars topica* leads to and makes possible the *ars critica*, and the *ars critica* in turn necessitates the *ars topica* as its own starting point. They, like the intellect and the imagination, are the two sides of the coin that is produced by philosophy. This interplay of the two sides that we find in the classics of the ancients and the moderns seems to decrease the closer we come to the major works of contemporary philosophy.

It is a disturbing sign of the times that late philosophical literature seems to lose much of the power of the word that is derived from the interplay of the discursive and the metaphorical. Perhaps grandness of thought goes against the current of the technological age. By Hegel's principle that philosophies are their own times apprehended in thoughts, we should perhaps expect nothing else but the disappearance of philosophy into the methods of its various schools, there to reside with the professionals. But it is a grim prospect, and one that the humanist philosopher must resist.

Irony and Taste

I have suggested how the Socratic question in philosophy is tied to the metaphor. Socrates also ties philosophy to the trope of irony. Philosophy shares metaphor with mythical narrative, but irony is the philosophical trope. Metaphor and irony generate meanings that are beyond the limits of discursive thought. They both require the power of ingenuity, or *ingenium*. *Ingenium* is required to grasp the connection between the components of the metaphor, and it is required to grasp in an irony how what is said literally is intended to imply a meaning beyond the literal. Irony is the presence of wit in philosophical works. Cicero says: "Irony, which they say was found in Socrates, and which he uses in the dialogues of Plato, Xenophon, and Aeschines, is a choice and clever way of speaking. It marks a man as free from conceit, and at the same time witty, when discussing wisdom, to deny it to himself and to attribute it playfully to those who make pretensions to it" (*Brutus, 292*).

With the question always comes the possibility of the trope of irony. Irony, like metaphor, involves the similarity of dissimilars, but in metaphorical formulation the connection is simply present. Irony presents the audience with what is not, rather than what is. The recipient of the ironic statement is not to take what is said in terms of what is in fact said, but in terms of the opposite of what is said. Things are other than what they seem. Vico says of irony that "it is fashioned of falsehood by dint of a reflection which wears the mask of truth."[19]

To penetrate the irony of a position is to form it as a question, to put it into question and then to be led beyond it to a meaning implied in its ironic state. The speech of the whole, the speech in which everything is to be told, must necessarily be a speech that encompasses oppositions. The speech of the whole is governed by the *coincidentia oppositorum*. It must pass through all opposites, great and small, near and far, particular and universal. It will be a series of ironic revelations, with each new beginning marked by the trope of metaphor and with each stage, each form of truth, held together by an overriding metaphor.

I have not until now taken any care to distinguish between the written and the spoken word in this consideration of philosophical language. In terms of the view I have developed, I suggest that proper philosophical speech is not only governed by the sense of the whole, the question, and the tropes of irony and metaphor, but it is, when written, an attempt to speak by writing. The written word is static, but the form of the question is dynamic. One might put it this way: philosophical writing is always a mask because its aim is to get its reader to the level of speaking, to get the reader to make in words the truth of the speech that is locked on the page.

In this sense, the written word points to the spoken word that is distinctive of philosophy's own Socratic origins.

Philosophical questions are not only put in language, they are also put to language. The philosopher is the maker of the word in the sense that the philosopher makes philosophy as a linguistic art. But the philosopher does not make language. Language always stands before the philosopher as a memory theater. It is like a theater because it provides the theater of thought itself, that scene in which the actions of philosophical thought can take place. It is a memory theater because each word carries with it the memory of the race. It masks a history of its own meaning. Philosophical speech, like humanist speech generally, must achieve what it wishes to convey by playing on the totality of the word. In the view suggested here, philosophy is made in the theater of language to which the philosopher comes, and which is set in motion by questions and by the ingenuity of metaphorical connections.

To say this is to take a stand against the notion that philosophical language is ever rightly technical. As Collingwood puts it: "The greatest philosophers, especially those who by common consent have written well in addition to thinking well, have used nothing that can be called a technical vocabulary."[20] Philosophical language is, to endorse another Socratic principle of speaking, the language of the agora. Philosophy itself becomes a mask because as Socrates uses the ordinary words of speech he can barely be understood; what is being said is at any moment possibly ironic and beyond our grasp. The philosopher is always in the position of putting questions to language because language seems to have all the answers. The way words are used or can allow themselves to be used contains all that the philosopher desires to know. As the possessor of language he is the immediate possessor of self-knowledge, in the sense of the collective experience of humanity that underlies the words and is carried in their unfathomable histories. In language lies, in a sense, all the answers to the philosopher's questions, yet language itself rests upon a distinction between thing and word. Language is not all there is and language is not simply about itself.

We are left to hold, with Plato, regarding the relation of philosophy to language, what he says in his *Seventh Letter:*

> In a word, it is an inevitable conclusion from this that when anyone sees anywhere the written work of anyone, whether that of a lawgiver in his laws or whatever it may be in some other form, the subject treated cannot have been his most serious concern—that is, if he is himself a serious man. His most serious interests have their abode somewhere in the noblest region of the field of his activity. If, however, he really was seriously concerned with these matters and put them in writing, "then surely" not the gods, but mortals "have utterly blasted his wits." (344c–d; compare *Iliad* 7.360, 12.234)

True philosophy is never written down. To think with the gods, the ancient occupation of philosophy, is to respect language as the power distinctive to human thought but not to trust it to embody wisdom fully. Language approaches wisdom when speech is eloquent, when the whole of the subject of the philosopher is spoken about and the subject, in this case, is not something specific, but is "all that there is."

The absence of irony in a philosophical work is as disturbing and unnatural as the absence of a sense of humor in a person, since, as mentioned earlier, laughter is one of the distinctive marks of the human. Oscar Wilde said all bad poetry is sincere. All bad philosophy is also sincere. A philosophy that lacks ironic sense is boring. It takes itself seriously in the extreme and in so doing loses the agility of thought that irony provides. Bertolt Brecht said that Hegel had "the stuff of one of the greatest humorists among philosophers; Socrates is the only other one who had a similar method," and he concludes: "I have never met a person without a sense of humor who has understood Hegel's dialectic."[21] Philosophies that are dialectical especially lend themselves to the use of irony. Cicero says that dialectic "may be looked upon as a contracted or compressed eloquence" (*Brutus*, 309). But irony is still to be found throughout non-dialectical philosophies in the history of philosophy: recall Descartes' aforementioned circular argument to the Faculty of Theology. With this ironic statement Descartes paves the way for founding modern philosophy.

A final word might be said about taste. Taste is the intangible but necessary standard that must guide the reader of the history of philosophy. Ezra Pound in *How to Read* says: "In each age one or two men of genius find something, and express it. It may be in only a line or two lines, or in some quality of cadence; and thereafter two dozen, or two hundred, or two or more thousand followers repeat and dilute and modify." Pound is thinking more about literature in general than philosophy, but his principle applies here. The reader who enters the world of the history of philosophy must cultivate the good eye. He must look for the rare act of philosophical genius that suddenly appears in a thinker's work, the act that carries with it an epiphany for the reader with a good eye. Once the statements that embody this genius are recognized, the whole sense of an age is opened up. Pound sees in this approach a new method of instruction. He says: "If the instructor would select his specimens from works that contain these discoveries and solely on the basis of discovery—which may lie in the dimension of depth, not merely of some novelty on the surface—he would aid his student far more than by presenting his authors at random, and talking about them *in toto*."[22]

Taste—the ability to perceive the real discoveries in thought—is the key to the canon of great works that each reader must form. The danger in this approach is what Vico, in his oration *On the Study Methods of Our Time*, said was his greatest fear, that "of being alone in wisdom; this kind of solitude exposes one to the danger of becoming either a god or a fool."[23] Being alone in wisdom is the risk the real reader and the real instructor must take. The alternative is to learn nothing from the works in the history of philosophy, by treating them all the same, as simply items in a curriculum.

The key to entering those works that contain real discoveries is to pursue a threefold method of reading. As Cicero says, "Reading is the wellspring of perfect eloquence" (*Brutus*, 322), and eloquence, as has been said, requires speaking on the whole of a subject, not just speaking in fine words. A perfect method of reading is to read the work first as a whole to grasp its general meaning, then to read it with attention to its various parts and the transitions of thought that combine them, and finally to read it for the turns of phrase, for the style in which the thoughts are presented.[24] Style, from *stilus*, the instrument with which one writes, comes to mean how one writes. Whitehead says that style "is the last acquirement of the educated mind"; it is "the ultimate morality of mind."[25] Manner of expression is what impresses the memory and allows the reader to hold in mind the content of the thought. All books can be read in this threefold way, especially those that need to be mastered for their great discoveries.

Finally, I suggest that books in the history of philosophy should be read not atomically, as though they were simply individual entities, but against each other, dialectically. Although there is great profit in comprehending how one work leads to another in the historical development of philosophical thought, there is also great importance in pairing the ancients against the moderns so as to consider their versions of truth and to consider in what sense a balance may be struck between them. The truest conception of the history of philosophy is that it remains a treasure-house containing the memory of what has been attempted in the love of wisdom. And in any new attempts at philosophical thought it is only decent and certainly wise to draw upon this treasure-house.

THE ORIGIN OF PHILOSOPHY
AND THE THEATER OF THE WORLD

All the world's a stage,
And all the men and women merely players;
They have their exits and their entrances.
     —William Shakespeare, *As You Like It*, 2.7.139–41

At the center of the study of the history of philosophy is the question of who the philosopher is. The remarks which follow offer one way of viewing this question, making use of the history of philosophy to pursue an answer.

The Pythagorean Coining of the Word *Philosopher*

Heraclides of Pontus, who likely acted as head of the Academy during Plato's third Sicilian journey, in a medical dialogue concerning "the case of the woman whose breathing had stopped," relates the coining of the word *philosopher* by Pythagoras.[1] This dialogue concerns the apotheosis of Empedocles, who, having attained wisdom, demonstrated his divinity by resurrecting the woman from a state of death, or near death, to life by taking into account what ordinary physicians had ignored—her soul. The true physician must comprehend the universe and know the truth of human nature as a whole.

Heraclides, originally a member of the Platonic Academy and later associated with the Lyceum, was a prolific and elegant writer with a Pythagorean bias. His relation of the scene in which Pythagoras coins the word *philosopher* appears at first glance to be a digression in his dialogue, unconnected to the scene of the resurrection of the unconscious woman. The dialogue itself does not survive, and our fullest account of this part of it is in Cicero's *Tusculan Disputations* (4.3). Cicero says that philosophy in the sense of wisdom is something very ancient, but the name is of recent origin. Wisdom as the knowledge of things divine and human goes back to the seven sages, who were called *sophoi* by the Greeks, and further back to Lycurgus, and even to the heroic age, to Ulysses and Nestor.

The stories, Cicero says, of Atlas holding up the sky or Prometheus chained to the Caucasus, or Cepheus being turned into a star, could not have arisen if these ancients had not possessed a superhuman knowledge of heavenly things. This tradition of wisdom came down to the time of Pythagoras, who, according to Heraclides, visited Phlius, the chief town of a small district of northeastern Peloponnesus usually allied with Sparta. There Pythagoras engaged in a conversation on certain learned subjects with Leon, the tyrant of the Phliasians. Leon, impressed with Pythagoras's genius and eloquence, asked him what art he professed. Pythagoras replied that he knew no special art, but was a philosopher. Leon wondered at the novelty of the word *philosopher* and asked Pythagoras what philosophers were and how they differed from other men.

Pythagoras likened life to the Great Games at Olympia, in which some come to compete for glory, some to conduct business for profit and gain, and some, the noblest of all, to spectate, to see what occurs and how. Pythagoras said it is as if we have migrated from a different mode of life and being into this one, as if from a city to a crowded festival, in which some are slaves to fame and others to financial fortune, but in which there are some rare spirits who hold all else as nothing and who contemplate the nature of things. These give themselves the name "lovers of wisdom." As at the festival it most becomes one to be a spectator, so in life contemplation and comprehension of the nature of things surpasses all other pursuits. So Cicero reports.

A second but similar version of the three lives is given in Iamblichus's *Life of Pythagoras*, emphasizing the sense in which the philosopher commands a wisdom that contemplates the nature of number and of the reasons (*logoi*) which prove everything, and that this pursuit of wisdom requires erudition (12). Diogenes Laertius, referring to the dialogue of Heraclides, claims that Pythagoras, in his answer to Leon, said that he was not wise. He said that only the gods possessed wisdom (*sophia*), that he was a lover of wisdom (*Lives of Eminent Philosophers*, 1.12; see also 8.8). This comment of Diogenes suggests that Pythagoras, in his exchange with Leon, likely engaged in a wordplay on *sophia* and *philia*. The adjective *philo-* (from *philein*, "to love," or *philos*, "beloved," "loving"), when joined to a noun, can characterize a person in whose life the thing designated by the noun plays a decisive role. By joining *philo-* to *sophos*, Pythagoras removes himself from the gods, who do have wisdom as a divine possession, and from the class of *sophoi* or sages, who claim wisdom as a human possession. *Philia* (from *philos*) has the connotation that one is attached to wisdom as one is attached to a friend. As there is no particular art or skill (*téchnē*) associated with friendship, so there is none to be associated with philosophy. Pythagoras's reply to Leon hides the fact that to be a lover of wisdom is in some sense to be wise. In order to love wisdom one must in some sense already possess it, or one would not know if it merited such attachment.

Pythagoras's reply allows him to avoid a conflict with Leon. As tyrant, Leon's power is absolute. If Pythagoras is wise in the sense of possessing a particular art or skill, then he commands something that Leon does not. Leon's art is that of acquiring and keeping power—the art of politics—and he takes the polis as the absolute ground of human concern. Pythagoras, if he is wise, would possess what the gods possess. He would, like Empedocles, be divine or nearly divine. This would place Pythagoras in a very dangerous position with Leon. He would possess that to which Leon has no access. By claiming himself a *philosophos,* a lover of wisdom, Pythagoras appears harmless, a spectator. The coining of the word *philosophy* establishes the philosopher's relation to the state. Pythagoras confronts Leon in a mask—saying what philosophy is by claiming to say what it is not.

Logically, Pythagoras's coining of *philosophy* and *philosopher* combines a stipulative and a lexical definition. Pythagoras stipulates a meaning, but he does so by combining two terms whose meaning is already established, making them carry a precise meaning in a new way. Rhetorically, Pythagoras's coining is accomplished by an ironic speech, making philosophy the noblest of pursuits and lives and at the same time making it appear harmless to the city. Definition is oration. Pythagoras's speech is the mask behind which all true philosophy is done.

The tale of the origin of the name and nature of philosophy by Heraclides is not a digression in his dialogue. The medical theme of his work is only incidental; it is actually a discourse on wisdom. Its point is the divinity of Empedocles, who is wise and who thus shares wisdom with the gods. Where human wisdom has failed to resurrect the woman whose breathing has stopped, Empedocles' divine wisdom prevails and allows him to grasp the nature of the soul (psyche) and affect a cure. Performing such a miracle is dangerous because it is threatening to the tyrant. It is beyond the scope of the tyrant's power and would cause him to desire to ally with such supernatural power in order to extend his own. Pythagoras's mask of ironic speech provides the philosopher a place to stand by fixing the nature of the philosopher between the gods and man.

The Socratic Philosopher's Dilemma

Philosophy undergoes a redefinition by the Platonic Socrates. In his analogy of three lives, Pythagoras portrays the philosopher as a spectator of the universe. The philosopher's object is all that is in the world and all that is in the heavens. Socrates shifts the lover of wisdom's object from nature to human nature. This reconception of philosophy lands Socrates in the Athenian court and then in prison. The last hours before his death are the subject of the *Phaedo*. On his way back home to Elis after Socrates' death Phaedo stops at Phlius, where he reports on it to a group of Pythagoreans who have settled there since their expulsion from Croton in southern Italy (57a). Socrates' two main discussants, Simmias and Cebes, are from Thebes, where other members of the Pythagorean brotherhood have settled under the leadership of Philolaus. The *Phaedo* takes up the Pythagorean themes of immortality and reincarnation, which are not present in this way in the *Euthyphro*, *Apology*, or *Crito*. What easily goes unnoticed is that the account of Socrates' death in Athens is given in Phlius, where philosophy was first defined. Pythagoras did not follow the wisdom of his own stance in relation to Leon, and on taking up politics in Croton he either fled with his followers or was killed by the Crotonites. Plato yielded to a similar temptation in his journeys to Syracuse, to the courts of Dionysus I and II, finally escaping with his life.

In the *Phaedo* the nature of philosophy is conveyed in two ways: in what Socrates, as the archetypal philosopher, does—how he acts, what he is—and in what Socrates says the nature of the philosopher and of philosophy is. Socrates says: "Those who philosophize rightly are practicing to die" (*hoi orthos philosophountes apothneskein meletosi;* 67e3–4). This is emphasized again later in the dialogue, where Socrates is describing the soul. He characterizes philosophy when pursued in the right way as "practice of death" (*melete thanatou;* 81a1–2). We philosophize because we are mortal. Neither gods nor nonhuman animals have need of philosophy because for them the fact of their existence is not a problem. They ask no questions.

In explaining the connection of philosophy to mortality, Socrates says that the philosopher is not resentful of death because he knows that pure knowledge cannot be found in this life. He says: "Any man whom you see resenting death was not a lover of wisdom but a lover of the body, and also a lover of wealth or of honors, either or both" (*Phaedo*, 68b–c). This distinction between the lover of the body and the lover of wisdom reflects Pythagoras's three lives, honor being the object of spirited deeds and wealth being useful to satisfy the appetites. In the *Republic* these lives are reflected in the tripartite division of the soul—the appetitive, spirited, and rational. All but the philosopher regard death as a great evil.

Socrates says the greatest danger the philosopher faces is to lose attachment to reasonable discourse. No greater misfortune could befall anyone than to develop a dislike for logos. Socrates says that "we should not become misologists, as people become misanthropes" (*Phaedo*, 89d). Add to this Cebes' claim that "any man who faces death with confidence is foolish, unless he can prove that the soul is altogether immortal" (88b). Socrates spends his last day in discourse with Simmias and Cebes on the nature and immortality of the soul. The exchange between them finally leads to Socrates' relation of a myth of the afterlife, like the *Republic*'s myth of Er and the myth of the soul's survival after death in the *Gorgias*.

The arguments about the immortality of the soul are an irony. We have the figure of Socrates doing what he always was doing, right to the end, but the arguments are all inconclusive (see *Phaedo*, 107a–b). In a final irony, Socrates uncovers his head and says his last words: "Crito, we owe a cock to Asclepius. See to it, and don't forget" (118a). Then he pulls the cover back over his head, and in a wink he is gone. Socrates leaves his companions and us with a joke. Asclepius is the god of healing. The standard view is that Socrates means death to be the cure for life. But this view does not do justice to the scene.

Asclepius was more than a miraculous worker of cures. He also succeeded in restoring the dead to life, an act for which Zeus struck him dead with a thunderbolt—for restoration of the dead was a thwarting of the natural order. Could Socrates' choice to sacrifice a cock to Asclepius have also been a reference to Aristophanes' use of the example of a cock, in *The Clouds*, to satirize Socrates' manner of discourse? In the *Apology* Socrates cites Aristophanes and his comedy as a source for the shaping of public opinion against him (18c–19c; cf. *Phaedo*, 70b). The word *cock* (*alektruōn*) Socrates uses in his request to Crito is the same as that used by Aristophanes in *The Clouds*, in his spoof of Socrates' lesson to Strepsiades on profound speaking (660–65; compare 845–55).

The cock, with its feathers and beak, is the ancient symbol, in consciousness, of the fool. Crito, the faithful but not the brightest of Socrates' followers, takes him seriously, acting as the straight man in Socrates' tragic-comedic scene. Socrates has been joking with Crito all along, answering his question of where they should bury him by saying he can bury him any way he would like if he can catch him, once he is dead. Socrates is convicted of irreligion, yet, ironically, his last request is for a religious observance. We cannot help but be moved by Socrates' death scene each time we read it. It is not simply comedic. Like philosophy itself, the scene is tragic-comedic. Socrates, the human figure of philosophy, is a tragic hero, an example of heroic mind in the theater of the world. Essential to the Socratic mentality is the ironic sense of life. The philosopher's wisdom is both beyond and within the human comedy.

The cock is a characteristic sacrifice to Asclepius. The reason for this is the association of Asclepius with the sunrise, his father having been Apollo, the sun god. The cock crows at dawn. The morning song of Asclepius was incised in marble in the Asclepieion at Athens, on the southern slope of the Acropolis. Socrates' death is a birth in death, in the way that the sunrise is a birth in the dark of the night. Socrates' last words to Crito have less to do with the traditional interpretation of death being a cure for life than with the Asclepian hymn to the sunrise. Socrates is saying the light is coming, let us give thanks.[2]

In the *Cratylus* Socrates says, in accord with Hesiod and the poets, that when a good man dies he becomes a daemon, "which is a name given to him because it accords with wisdom" (398c).

Daemons are said, in the *Apology* (27d–e), to be gods or the children of gods, and in the *Symposium* (202e) to be messengers from the gods. Recall that Socrates was directed by his special light or voice, his *daimonion,* one of the references to which is in the *Apology* (31c7–d4 and 40a4). "Wisdom," Cicero says, "is the knowledge of things divine and human and acquaintance with the cause of each of them" (*Tusculan Disputations,* 4.26.57). Socrates in the *Apology* asserts that he may possess human wisdom (20d–e), but he also says—as did Pythagoras—that real wisdom is the property of the gods (23a). Socrates adds that he has been so busy in attempting to discover wisdom that he has had no time for politics (23b). To deny being wise is to be wise, and to deny the possession of divine wisdom is at least to know what it is. To know a thing one must know what it is and what it is not.

The two great ancient conceptions of philosophy are both associated with Phlius. In the *Protrepticus* Aristotle says, of Pythagoras, "Then what is it among existing things for the sake of which nature and god have brought us into being? Pythagoras, when asked about this, answered, 'To observe the heavens,' and used to say that he was an observer of nature and had come to life for the sake of this."[3] Of Socrates, Cicero says: "Socrates was the first to call philosophy down from the heavens and set her in the cities of men and bring her also into their homes and compel her to ask questions about life and morality and things good and evil" (*Tusculan Disputations,* 5.4.10–11). To call philosophy down from the heavens Socrates required the device of the question. The question makes possible a new sense of wisdom. To formulate questions is distinctively human (see chapter 4). It makes being into a problem, and when being becomes a problem, being can be grasped as a principle rather than as a visible thing. As a principle it becomes accessible to thought, to reason, and to language, although its nature can never be fully said in words. Socrates avoids politics but is tempted enough by it to become its gadfly and for his efforts suffers its wrath.

The ancient development of philosophy leads to what we may call *the philosopher's dilemma*, which is as follows:

> If the philosopher loves what men possess, then the philosopher loves politics; and if the philosopher loves what the gods possess, then the philosopher loves wisdom. The philosopher must love either what men possess or what the gods possess. Thus the philosopher must love either politics or wisdom.

Philosophers who love politics are lovers of the body, seekers of wealth or honor, as if these were absolutes. To such philosophers we might apply the term "foolosophers," "foolers" of wisdom (*morosophoi*; from *sophos*, "wise," and *moros*, "foolish"), coined by the first English translator of Erasmus.[4] Their folly is to believe that the life of the mind is to be found in the polis, and their speech is directed not to justice but to social justice, not to *sōphrosynē* (moderation) but to excess, not to courage but to rights, not to wisdom but to information, and not to the good but to the social good. Yet the philosopher lives in the human world and the human world is governed by politics. What, then, is the philosopher's role in this anti-philosophical world, this world of injustice, intemperance, cowardice, ignorance, and evil?

The Renaissance Humanist Theater of the World

For perspective on this problem we may turn to the Renaissance and early modern idea of the *theatrum mundi*, the "theater of the world." In Descartes' *Cogitationes Privatae* we come upon this declaration: "Just as actors are warned not to allow shame [*pudor*] to appear on their brows, and thus put on a mask: so I, about to step upon the theater of the world [*mundi theatrum*], where I have so far been a spectator, come forward in a mask."[5]

Theatrum, from the Greek *theatron* (*theasthai,* "to see," "to view"), is akin to *thauma,* "wonder." The theater has a connection to that passion which Descartes understood as "a sudden surprise of the soul which brings to its attention objects that seem unusual and extraordinary,"[6] and which Aristotle said, in the *Metaphysics,* is the beginning of philosophy: "For it is owing to their wonder that men both now begin and at first began to philosophize" (982b12–13). Among the meanings of *theatrum,* in the Middle Ages, were a place of assembly and a marketplace where goods for sale were laid out. The Athenian agora, where Socrates practiced philosophy, fits this description well.

The "theater of the world" of the sixteenth and seventeenth centuries, as a simile of human life, has its precedents in the ancient Neoplatonists and the Stoics. A very early sense of the theater of the world is expressed by the Cynic-Stoic Aristo of Chios, who, to illustrate his doctrine of a life of perfect indifference to everything, adhering neither to virtue nor vice, compared the wise man (*sophos*) "to a good actor, who, if called upon to take the part of a Thersites or of an Agamemnon, will impersonate them both becomingly" (Diogenes Laertius, *Lives of Eminent Philosophers,* 7.160). Among the Neoplatonists, Plotinus likens the roles played in human life to those of characters in a play. He says: "But the actors [in the universal drama] have something extra, in that they act in a greater space than that within the limits of a stage" (*Enneads,* 3.2.17). It is Providence that arranges the roles in the universal drama, "for each place is fitted to their characters, so as to be in tune with the rational principle of the universe, since each individual is fitted in, according to justice, in the parts of the universe designed to receive him" (ibid.). All is ordered in accord with rational proportion.

Among the later Stoics, Marcus Aurelius concludes his *Meditations* with a comparison of the stages of a life as lived to the acts of a play arranged by providential order. He says that we appear upon the stage of life and then, when it is time, depart (12.36). Epictetus, in the *Encheiridion,* or *Manual,* says: "Remember that you are an actor in a play, the character of which is determined by the Playwright: if He wishes the play to be short, it is short; if long, it is long" (17). You are to act the role you receive: "For this is your business, to play admirably the role assigned you" (ibid.). Cicero echoes this: "The actor, for instance, to please his audience need not appear in every act to the very end; it is enough if he is approved in the parts in which he plays; and so it is not necessary for the wise man to stay on this mortal stage to the last fall of the curtain" (*De Senectute*, 11.70).

The idea of the theater of the world is twofold. On the one hand the theater is seen as a microcosm of the world, a realization of Giordano Bruno's metaphysics of microcosm and macrocosm. This sense is a merging of the Christian idea of the heavenly theater with the Roman amphitheater.[7] Its principles are derived from the Roman architect Vitruvius, as reflected in Leon Battisti Alberti's *Ten Books on Architecture* and as reflected in the public theaters of London, especially the Globe Theatre, the site of Shakespeare's plays.[8] The theater as a theater of the world is a representation of the cosmos, in which actors play the roles of human life. On the other hand, the theater is a moral emblem which presents human life as a spectacle, governed by the human and the divine. It is present in book form in Robert Fludd's *Theatrum Vitae Humanae*, which is a series of moral and religious emblems accompanied by poems and discourses in Latin.[9] This connection of emblem and instruction in moral philosophy is similar to what Shaftesbury later attempts in his "noble virtuoso scheme of morals" in his unfinished *Second Characters*, written in Naples, a city in which daily life is a tableau and a theater.[10]

The theater of the world has a particular starting point in the conception of the theater of Giulio Camillo, who joined it with the art of memory. Camillo's *L'Idea del Theatro* was the idea of a theater of image-places (*pitture*), each on a mythical theme, set where the audience would usually be, in seven rows and seven grades, in an amphitheater. The spectator thus entered on the stage, and by viewing and comprehending this language and form of the divine *mens*, the results of all human memory, the student could acquire all of human knowledge.[11]

To make the theater a microcosm of the cosmos and human life is also to make the human world itself a theater. This is the approach of Plotinus and the great Stoics. It is the idea that the world is a theater and all lives within it are roles. This sense of life is behind Sebastian Brandt's *Narrenschiff,* Erasmus's *Praise of Folly,* Castiglione's *Book of the Courtier,* and books of manners, such as Stefano Guazzo's *L'Arte della Conversazione,* and even Boccaccio's *Decameron.* That the human world is a theater is the key to Renaissance moral philosophy. If this is so, what is the philosopher's role in this theater? An answer to this lies in the progression of three Renaissance thinkers: Marsilio Ficino, Pico della Mirandola, and Juan Luis Vives.

Ficino's famous letter in praise of philosophy (1476), sent to the Venetian orator and statesman Bernardo Bembo, ambassador to Florence, presents philosophy as the perfecter of man. The acme of each art and activity is reached when it touches philosophy. Ficino says: "Above all, Philosophy removes misery from mortals, and bestows happiness upon them." He says: "Nothing else is true happiness but true Philosophy, when it becomes in fact love of wisdom, as it is defined by the wise." And further, "With Philosophy as its guide, the soul gradually comes to comprehend with its intelligence the natures of all things, and entirely assumes their forms."[12]

In a second letter, to his lifelong friend Giovanni Cavalcanti, later in 1476, Ficino takes up the theme that "Philosophy does not teach us to live with princes; indeed she forbids it." Ficino says that in his previous letter he attempted to show that philosophy teaches all things. But, he says,

> I ought to have made the one exception, that she does not teach us how to live with princes. For if she forbids this altogether, as indeed she does, clearly she cannot teach us how.

She altogether forbids it, it seems to me, since she commands the opposite; for in discovering the love of truth she surely requires a tranquil mind and a free life. However, truth does not dwell in the company of princes; only lies, spiteful criticism and fawning flattery, men pretending to be what they are not and pretending not to be what they are.[13]

Ficino, of course, lives with princes, but at the letter's end he precludes the Medici (his patrons) from this criticism, saying that they are cultured princes, and of a higher order.

The end of philosophy is not politics but civil wisdom that is connected to divine wisdom.[14] Politics and civil wisdom should not be confused. Politics is the art of obtaining power and using it in human affairs or in the affairs of the state, where it has behind it war or the threat of war. Civil wisdom is the art of life, of which misanthropy is its opposite. At the level of the state, civil wisdom is the art of government by example and persuasion. When philosophy becomes unattached to civil wisdom and enters politics it becomes ideological, a form of thought based strictly on the passions and on the doctrine of power.

Civil wisdom, for the Renaissance humanists as well as for Cicero, is based on the interconnection between *sapientia, eloquentia,* and *prudentia* (*De Partitionibus Oratoriae,* 23.79). Eloquence, the ideal of the humanists, is wisdom speaking (*la sapienza che parla*). Eloquence, as Quintilian says, is the ability to speak wholly on a subject (*Institutio Oratoria,* 8.15–16), and as Giambattista Vico says, the "whole is really the flower of wisdom."[15] Prudence is the ability to act on the basis of wisdom put into words. *Prudentia* and *providentia* are synonyms. The prudent act in the human world is like the providential act of the divine in history. Prudence is wisdom in deed as eloquence is wisdom in word, as discussed in chapter 6 of this book. Vico says: "Having been imbued with the knowledge of divine things, may you learn prudence in human affairs, first the moral, which forms man, then the civil which forms the citizen."[16]

He further says: "There is only one 'art of prudence' and this art is philosophy," alluding to the *Digest* of Roman law, which claims that jurisprudence is true philosophy.[17]

To act prudently is not simply to act expediently. This is the notion of prudence (*Klugheit*) dictated by Kant and all others who would hold that proper human action is rule-governed and subject to universal criteria.[18] In this view, to act prudently is other than to act morally. In the humanist view, to act prudently is to act according to what is possible in terms of the particular situation. It is to act in accord with self-determination, which is based on character and virtue, on the harmony of the appetites, will, and intellect, directed to the good. The presence of the good connects prudent action to the divine, to what the gods love.

Prudent action presumes what the Florentine historian and statesman Francesco Guicciardini calls the "good eye," the *buono occhio*. He says: "All that which has been in the past and is at present will be again in the future. But both the names and the appearances of things change, so that he who does not have a good eye will not recognize them. Nor will he know how to grasp a norm of conduct or make a judgment by means of observation."[19] Another way to say this is Bacon's statement, as quoted by Jorge Luis Borges: "Solomon saith, 'There is no new thing upon the earth'; so that as Plato had an imagination, that all knowledge was but remembrance; so Solomon giveth his sentence, 'That all novelty is but oblivion.'"[20] Human wisdom is based on memory, as Camillo's theater demonstrates. To think well is to remember well. As Horace says, from right thoughts right words follow on naturally (*Ars Poetica*, 309–11). To think well is to speak well. To act well requires both of these as a basis.

How are wisdom and eloquence learned, that are required for prudence in human affairs, for the achievement of civil wisdom? The answer to this is found in Pico della Mirandola's "Oration on the Dignity of Man." Pico begins his oration by saying: "I have read in the records of the Arabians, reverend Fathers, that Abdala the Saracen [likely the cousin of Mohammed], when questioned as to what on this stage of the world, as it were, could be seen most worthy of wonder, replied: 'There is nothing to be seen more wonderful than man [*quid in hac quasi mundana scaena admirandum maxime spectaretur, nihil spectari homine admirabilius respondisse*].'"[21] Pico says this view is in agreement with the Hermetic tradition of the *Pimander* and the *Asclepius* and with David's claim in Psalms (8:5) that man is a little lower than the angels.

The wonder and dignity of man is derived from man's place between the divine and the natural worlds. The philosopher is the most wondrous of those who occupy this position. The true philosopher "is a heavenly being not of this earth."[22] The role of man on this "stage of the world," as Pico says, is to fulfill the Delphic precepts of "Nothing too much," which offers a rule for the pursuit of all the virtues in moral philosophy; "Know thyself," which encourages us to investigate all of nature, including human nature; and "Thou art," to attempt to grasp the divine. This three-fold philosophy contains the key to the dignity of man and to the community of philosophers.[23]

Pico's "Oration" leads to the Spanish humanist Juan Luis Vives's "Fable About Man." Vives defines man directly in terms of the theater of the world. He says: "Man is himself a fable and a play [*homo ipse ludus ac fabula est*]."[24] This takes us past Aristotle's definition of man as rational (*Topics*, 128a) and as a political animal (*Politics*, 1253a). But it recalls his definition of man in the *Poetics* in which man is called the imitative animal. "Imitation is natural to man from childhood, one of his advantages over the lower animals being this, that he is the most imitative creature in the world, and learns first by imitation" (1448b6–9). Aristotle also says that man is "the only animal that laughs" (*Parts of Animals*, 673a), a fact Socrates plays on in his final comedic scene.

The scene of Vives's fable is a play following a feast given by Juno on her birthday. She has asked Jupiter to arrange a play for the other gods to witness. Jupiter has arranged an amphitheater: "Uppermost, to wit in the skies, were the stalls and seats of the divine spectators; nethermost—some say in the middle—the earth was placed as a stage for the appearance of the actors, along with all the animals and everything else."[25] As the action develops, man emerges among all other creatures as the *archimimus,* the arch-mime, who proceeds to play all levels of beings. Man is able to don masks and imitate all things, including Jupiter himself "in his wisdom, prudence, memory."[26] Man is Jupiter's mime and becomes the delight of the gods, so much so that they invite man to assume a seat in their heavenly choir. The key to man discovering human nature and to prudence is man's ability to play all roles, to imitate all forms of being, from plants to animals to types of humans to gods, to Jupiter, assuming these identities by means of masks.

As Descartes says in the passage from his notebook quoted earlier, when the philosopher moves from the role of spectator to that of actor, he steps onto the theater of the world in a mask. Pythagoras is the spectator, but Socrates is the spectator at one moment and the actor at the next. We regard him at one moment and he is the theoretician, and yet at another he is the practician. Socrates is present in the activities of the agora, asking questions about those activities, yet he is never of the agora. He appears as a visitor who will stay for a while, give us something we need, and then depart. Like Plato's comment in the *Seventh Letter* (341c–d) that his philosophy was never written down (as discussed in chapter 4), Socrates never really says what his wisdom is. His doctrine is as much what he says as what he does.

The humanist philosopher enters into all the fields of the liberal arts and can penetrate every role in the theater of the world, like man himself. The humanist's love of wisdom is the love of the human and all that is human. Nothing human is foreign to him. His mimetic power allows him to enter into each role and grasp its inner form. The Neoplatonic humanists subscribe in various ways to Camillo's first sentence in his *L'Idea del Theatro:* "The most ancient and wisest writers have always had the habit of entrusting to their writings the secrets of God under obscure veils, so that they are not understood except by those who (as Christ says) have ears to hear, namely who by God are chosen to grasp his most sacred mysteries."[27] This is the principle reserved for the community of philosophers that Pico projects.

The Hegelian Theater of History

Bacon's fourth idol in his *New Organon* is the "Idol of the Theater." It designates erroneous views that come into the mind because of one's attachment to philosophical systems.[28] Philosophies are like stage-plays that place the mind in certain roles and that cause the world to be interpreted in terms of those roles. Bacon's fourth idol, besides its purpose in freeing the mind to make direct scientific observations and inductions from nature, transposes the *theatrum mundi* from a simile of the conduct of human affairs to one of the nature of philosophical systems. A philosophy of the whole is a theater of the world. The philosopher not only plays a role in the theater of the world, but the role the philosopher plays is the capturing of this world in thought and language. The theater of the world becomes the theater of thought. The self confronts itself.

The last grand figure of the theater of the world is Hegel. Hegel transforms the theater of the world into the theater of history. Hegel's stage set is not Phlius, Athens, or Florence; it is all of history as seen first from his university post in Jena. The philosopher acts not in the static structure of the city but in the historical world of nations at war and in peace—what Vico, following Augustine, calls "the great city of the human race."[29]

To master history is to master time. Hegel, in the *Phenomenology of Spirit*, intends to make time into a system, which is the form of philosophical truth. He says: "To help bring philosophy closer to the form of Science, to the goal where it can lay aside the title '*love* of knowing' and be *actual* knowing—that is what I have set myself to do."[30] In each of the stages of Hegel's *Phenomenology* consciousness plays out a role, each one unable to portray successfully the absolute nature of things, to grasp the true which is the whole. The fate of each stage is to be superseded by a next and more elaborate role that consciousness sets for itself.

Within the course of the experience of consciousness in the *Phenomenology,* Hegel introduces the appearance of the self as an I, as consciousness realizing it has an inner being, in terms of the raising of a curtain (*Vorhang*) in a theater. The stage-curtain is drawn away and there before the audience of the "we" and consciousness itself is the I, "gazing into the inner world."[31] In Hegel's *Phenomenology* the self-conscious self makes its appearance on a stage. Self-knowledge is not achieved by direct introspection but by the self playing each one of its possible roles in Hegel's necessary sequence of roles in the attainment of absolute knowing. "Spirit," as Hegel says, "necessarily appears in Time."[32]

At the stage of absolute knowing, the whole of things can be seen as a bacchanalian revel at which not a member is sober, but seen from this ultimate vantage point it is just as much a scene of transparent, unbroken calm in which each member has met its fate of falling straightaway into the others. The philosopher passes from a love of wisdom to a state of actual wisdom by passing through time to a point where the true is the whole (*Das Wahre ist das Ganze*). The whole is where time stands still. Hegel says absolute knowing is recollection, or *Erinnerung.* His emphasis is on "inwardness" or "innerness," conveyed by the German word *Erinnerung.* Hegel plays on this sense of "inner" by hyphenating *Er-innerung.*[33]

The philosopher who has acquired the science of wisdom can, through *Erinnerung,* enter into all of the revel, into each of its scenes, while at the same time not being of them. In the myth of Er at the end of the *Republic,* the souls, after their journey under the earth, are reborn and must choose their new lives. Their choice is affected by the spindle of Necessity in accordance with which all the revolutions of the heavens occur. Plato asks if we are all not in this position that the souls now find themselves: "So everywhere and always to choose the better [lives] from among those that are possible" (618b). This choice requires the wisdom of comprehending all the types of lives that philosophy can give. Only the wise have the experience to choose well.

Hegel says that what is recollected at the level of absolute knowing is a gallery of images or pictures (*Galerie von Bildern*)— all the stages or roles consciousness can play, all the scenes and subscenes of the great revel of the whole.[34] In the fragment called the "Earliest System-Program of German Idealism," Hegel advocates a "mythology of Reason" (*Mythologie der Vernunft*).[35] The *Phenomenology* is his fulfillment of this aim. The *Bild* (image) is the necessary access to the *Begriff* (concept). For Hegel, *spectating*, which is tied originally by Pythagoras to the love of wisdom, becomes *speculation*. The Platonic anamnesis becomes the Hegelian *Erinnerung*. Speculation accomplishes "seeing into" the object, into its inner being. It requires, Hegel says, the "speculative sentence" (*spekulativer Satz*), the philosophical proposition which, like Hegel's system itself, is a circle.[36] In this sentence the subject finds its meaning in the predicate and the predicate, to retain its meaning, must turn back to recollect the meaning as it began in the subject of the sentence. The speculative sentence is Hegel's answer to the false philosophy of what he calls "our literal-minded philosophers" (*unsere Buchstabenphilosophen*).[37]

All great books of philosophy—those that make wisdom their goal—are portraits of the philosophical life. Their purpose is to say what philosophy is, while saying what all else is, and to provide a guide to the philosopher's role in the world. "The kind of philosophy a man chooses," Fichte says, "depends upon the kind of man he is. For a philosophic system is no piece of dead furniture one can acquire and discard at will. It is animated with the spirit of the man who possesses it."[38]

Hegel sums up the role of the philosopher in the preface to his last book, the *Philosophy of Right*, in his famous dictum: "When philosophy paints its grey in grey, then is a shape of life grown old, and with grey in grey it cannot be rejuvenated, but only recognized; the owl of Minerva takes flight only at the falling of the dusk."[39] (See the further discussion of this image in chapter 6.) In an early treatise, written prior even to the *Phenomenology,* "The Scientific Ways of Treating Natural Law," Hegel described the history of the world as a great tragedy of ethical life in which the divine or the absolute is constantly performing with itself, giving birth to itself only to perish and then to rise again, a view reminiscent of Vico's—and James Joyce's—cycles of history.[40]

Ernst Cassirer says in *The Myth of the State:* "In Hegel's philosophy the Spinozistic formula *Deus sive natura* was converted into the formula *Deus sive historia*."[41] The divine as reason becomes history itself. Providence is the "cunning of reason" (*List der Vernunft*) present in the theater of history. In Vives's performance, the gods are seated in Jupiter's amphitheater to observe man's prowess as arch-mime. In Hegel's history, the divine realizes itself in events as consciousness realizes itself as capable of absolute knowing by playing all of the roles of its stages. Cassirer says further: "To Hegel the state is not only the representative but the very incarnation of the 'spirit of the world.' While St. Augustine regarded the *civitas terrena* as a distortion and disfigurement of the *civitas divina,* Hegel saw in this *civitas terrena* the 'Divine Idea as it exists on earth.' This is an entirely new type of absolutism."[42]

In the theater of history the philosopher's aim is to grasp and remember what has happened. This is the wisdom of Minerva. The philosopher's ability to "think and see," as Bacon would say, is based on the philosopher's sight at dusk.[43] The twilight of dusk is the same as the first light of the rosy-fingered dawn. The philosopher as the seer of the conclusion of the day is also the seer of the new day, a birth in death. As the master of time, the philosopher's recollection of what was produces a wisdom that includes what is to come. Minerva's knowledge depends upon Mnemosyne (Memory). Hegel calls Mnemosyne "the absolute Muse."[44] Only in this way does the philosopher escape politics, that which would rob philosophy of its power to know and its power to show the way to prudent action in the world.

Finally: what, then, is the philosopher's role in the theater of history? This is the question Cassirer set for himself in his inaugural lecture at the University of Göteborg, Sweden, in 1935, after he, as a Jew, had fled Germany. Cassirer quotes Albert Schweitzer's Olaus-Petri lectures, delivered at the University of Uppsala between the world wars, in 1922. Schweitzer said that philosophy cannot be blamed for the state of the world in these times. But philosophy can be blamed for the fact that it did not follow its ultimate vocation. He said: "In accordance with its ultimate vocation philosophy is the guide and caretaker of reason in general." Philosophy, from its unique perspective, should have notified us of the threat to our cultural ideals. Schweitzer concluded: "But in the hour of peril the watchman slept, who should have kept watch over us."[45] Cassirer says that because of his own concentration on theoretical philosophy in these years he does not exclude himself from this charge, and neither should we.

The role of the philosopher in the theater of history is the watchman. The mind's eye can see beyond politics and let us join spectating with the speculative. Spectating takes the philosopher to the edge of the theater, to the divine position of the audience, where speculation can take place. Speculation is the divine vision that all that is human is a circle, that all human affairs are circular, as memory teaches. From speculation comes the sagacity of the watchman, who sees with a providential eye history's course of good and evil and incites prudence, which produces civil wisdom. For what happens in the theater of the world, as I have suggested, is always a twice-told tale.

TWO VIEWS OF HISTORY
AND THE HISTORY OF PHILOSOPHY

to steal our historic presents
from the past postpropheticals . . .
——James Joyce, *Finnegans Wake,* 11.30

The Philosophy of History in the Grand Manner

The history of philosophy is part of history. The view one has of the history of philosophy depends upon the philosophy of history one holds. The modern founder of the philosophy of history is Giambattista Vico.[1] Less than a century later G. W. F. Hegel, unaware of Vico, began to present his lectures on the philosophy of history and the history of philosophy.[2] Vico and Hegel offer divergent views of history that entail two approaches to the comprehension of the history of philosophy. They represent the two major conceptions of historical time—time as cyclic and time as a total progression of events.

I do not intend the remarks that follow as more than very broad characterizations of Vico's and Hegel's approaches to history. Their views are the philosophy of history done in the grand manner. As Ernst Cassirer puts it: "It is this 'palingenesis,' this rebirth of the past, which marks and distinguishes the great historian."[3] Not all philosophy of history is addressed to the question of what all of history means. Much contemporary work in the philosophy of history is concerned with purely methodological questions: whether there are historical laws; how explanations in history differ from those in the natural or social and behavioral sciences; the epistemological status of historical objects; and so on.[4] The philosophy of history pursued in this fashion does not generate, nor does it intend to generate, a doctrine of the nature of the history of philosophy, as do philosophies of history in the grand manner.

My aim is to consider what Vico's and Hegel's general doctrines of history imply for an overall view of the history of philosophy. The student of the philosophical canon must at some point face the question of what the history of philosophy is as a whole. Pivotal for the differences between Vico and Hegel, I think, is how we are to regard the Renaissance philosophy of Italian humanism. Taking this as a test case, we can see how different philosophies of history produce different assessments of the importance of different periods of philosophy. How can Renaissance humanism be understood in terms of the conceptions of history found in Vico and Hegel? This presumes that "the Renaissance" is not a fixed period or a fixed historical idea that is in some way closed to consideration or reconsideration of its meaning. The Renaissance is a diverse period, as can be seen from its outline in chapter 3. It is generally humanistic, but my focus in what follows is specifically on the tradition of Italian humanism.

The "Renaissance" is subject to historiographical rethinking in the sense that history itself is subject to rethinking by any generation or philosophy of history. I take "history" (Latin *historia*, Greek *historia*) in its root sense of *historein*, "to inquire into, to examine, to relate." History, then, is a kind of knowing or judging (akin to Greek *idein*, "to see"), an act of human wit that can produce a methodical narrative of events, the writing of which is historiography. Those who pursue such narrative inquiry or judgments in which particulars are selected from authentic materials and synthetically brought together through critical principles are philosophers of history. Vico and Hegel are among those who pursue the whole of history. As Hegel says, "the true is the whole" and as Vico says, "the whole is the flower of wisdom." How does the Renaissance fit into these respective "wholes"? And which of these offers the most?

Vico and Hegel are *logopoioi*, "tellers of tales." Unlike contemporaries of Herodotus such as Scylax and Xanthus, they tell their tales not from voyages and observations of foreign customs and countrysides, but from their meditations on history. But like these early writers of narrative prose they write of gods, heroes, and men, and like them they profess to offer a true version of historical events. Vico and Hegel profess a scientific, at least in their own senses of science, rather than a poetic account of human activities. Both make this clear in the titles of their major works: Vico's *New Science* and Hegel's *System of Science,* part 1 of which he claimed was his *Phenomenology of Spirit,* which he also called the "Science of the Experience of Consciousness."

Vico's great tale is the story of the "course and recourse the nations run" (the *corsi* and *ricorsi*) in the "great city of the human race." Hegel's great tale is the "gallery of pictures" (*Galerie von Bildern*) of the *Phenomenology,* as he calls it at the end of the work, in which each picture or stage of consciousness leads progressively to the next. This sense of a total progression of the stages of human consciousness provides the basis for Hegel's telling of a single story of the history of philosophy and of a philosophy of human history in his lectures.

These grand tales that Vico and Hegel tell are full of smaller tales that each tells of the sights he sees. The label of "science" that each gives to his account is both metaphorical and ironic, seen in relation to the mathematical sciences of the seventeenth century of Vico's day and the experimental sciences of the nineteenth century of Hegel's. Each philosopher gives us a single metaphor through which history can be understood. Vico claims that there is an "ideal eternal history" (*storia ideale eterna*), a common pattern of three ages that each nation displays in its rise, development, and fall. Hegel claims that there is a "cunning of reason" (*List der Vernunft*) that operates within all events to make them a single, intelligible progression. Each ironically calls this total, speculative sense of thinking "science," as opposed to that modern, literal sense of the term. Those who would identify philosophy with the mathematical and empirical ordering of experience Hegel calls "our literal-minded philosophers" (*unsere Buchstabenphilosophen*) who are full of nothing but "healthy common sense" (*gesunder Menschenverstand*),[5] and Vico says that such concern with clarity, when used as the basis of philosophy, is only to see by "lamplight at night."[6]

Although Vico is the founder of the philosophy of history, he has no explicit theory of what today is called the Renaissance. Vico's philosophy itself, however, has been seen as an extension and culmination of Renaissance thought. Karl-Otto Apel called Vico the owl of Minerva of Italian Renaissance humanism.[7] Ernesto Grassi has made a similar observation.[8] Grassi has connected Vico's conception of philosophy with such humanist thinkers as Pico, Petrarch, Salutati, Landino, Poliziano, Vives, and Valla.[9] Eugenio Garin makes some similar remarks about Vico in connection with Pico and Ficino and the general development of humanism in his *L'Umanesimo Italiano,* but in other writings he also sees Vico as a thinker of his own time.[10] Garin says that the astrological sense of the cycle in the heavens, that all things will be made anew and rise again, runs as a theme through the centuries of the Renaissance, from the writings of Campanella up to Vico.[11]

Philosophical questioning of the nature of history does not begin with Vico. It is a topic of ancient thought from Herodotus and Thucydides down to the present, and it was never more vigorously discussed than in the Renaissance.[12] Vico is not the founder of the question: what is history? He is the founder of the philosophy of history as a special field of philosophy. Hegel never mentions Vico in his works, and there is no evidence that he had any knowledge of Vico. Vico can be connected to Herder, but not Hegel.[13]

Hegel is the founder of the history of philosophy. Interest in the history of philosophy existed from ancient times in the form of studies of the lives of great philosophers that begin with Aristotle's account of his predecessors. There is the study of the works of the ancients by the Renaissance humanists, the general quarrel between the ancients and the moderns, of which Vico was a part, and the later production of histories of certain schools of ancient thought developed by their modern exponents, as well as Jakob Brucker's famous five-volume *Critical History of Philosophy* of the mid-eighteenth century. There is a history of philosophy implicit in Vico. But Hegel is the founder of the history of philosophy as a completely connected history in which all philosophies find their place in a total, developmental conception of historical periods. Hegel lectured nine times on the history of philosophy in his career. The first time, at Jena in 1805–6, was in the same period as his preparation of the *Phenomenology*. It was at this time that he most fully wrote out the text of these lectures. The history of philosophy, for Hegel, is divided into Greek philosophy, the philosophy of the Middle Ages, and modern philosophy, ending, as might be expected, with the achievements of German philosophy.

What would now be called the Renaissance is treated by Hegel as a final section of the Middle Ages. In this section mention is made of Pico, Ficino, the Platonic Academy, and the revival of forms of Epicurean and Stoic thought and Ciceronian "popular philosophy," which Hegel says "has no real speculative value" but has some interest for general culture. Cardano is mentioned, and so is Campanella; there is a discussion of some of Bruno's ideas and also a section on Ramus, between which there is a discussion of the moral philosophy of Vanini (a figure regarded as quite minor today) because, Hegel says, Vanini's ideas have similarities with Bruno's and because they both were burned at the stake. Hegel treats this period in the history of philosophy as simply a transition, and his remarks are nearly random and certainly brief. He does, however, see this period as based on a revival of the studies of the ancients and a revival of the "sciences" that mark the end of Scholasticism. But he sees this as a period of thinkers falling between the Scholastics and the Reformation and then passes on to Francis Bacon and Jacob Boehme, whom he sees as the first modern philosophers.

Cassirer's Key to the Renaissance

Ernst Cassirer begins *The Individual and the Cosmos in Renaissance Philosophy* with a gloss on Hegel's famous dictum in the preface to the *Philosophy of Right* that just as any individual is a child of his time, "so is philosophy also *its own time comprehended in thoughts.*"[14] Neither an individual nor a philosophy, Hegel holds, can escape its own time, any more than one can jump over Rhodes. Cassirer claims that at first glance the work of Renaissance philosophers does not seem to illustrate Hegel's dictum of philosophy being simply its own time comprehended in thoughts. Cassirer says that the new spirit and new life associated with the Renaissance seems manifest in poetry, the visual arts, politics, and historical life, but not in philosophy. But Cassirer claims that a version of Hegel's dictum does hold true if we regard the individual thinkers of the Renaissance as elements in the systematic apprehension of its total spirit. (See the introduction to Renaissance philosophy in the outline in chapter 3.)

In his work on the logic of the "cultural sciences" (*Kulturwissenschaften*), Cassirer employs Jacob Burckhardt's concept of "man of the Renaissance" as an example of concept formation in the humanities as opposed to the formation of concepts in the natural sciences.[15] In a mathematically formed scientific concept, the place of any individual element in a series is fully determined by the general principle through which the series is ordered. Unlike this form of fully determinate ordering of individual elements, individual figures such as Leonardo da Vinci, Ficino, Machiavelli, and others point to the composite general principle or concept of "man of the Renaissance," which does not fully determine the nature of any one of them as particular historical individuals aligned under it. But a concept such as "man of the Renaissance" signifies the unity toward which any particular instance of the concept tends. Unlike scientific concepts of natural phenomena, the individual cannot be assigned a specific place within a fully determinate, logical order and system of concepts.

Why is Cassirer surprised, on approaching the Renaissance, that Hegel's dictum of the relationship of philosophy to its time does not appear to hold? I think it is because Hegel identifies philosophy with *Wissenschaft* ("science") and *Wissenschaft* with system. To philosophize, for Hegel, is to build a total system of experience. That system or totality of thought will be a reflection of what is present in the time of the philosopher who builds it. Each individual philosopher, to be considered a philosopher, must be the producer of a system. Although the philosopher is in a sense above his time, he is not beyond it. He is a child of his time in the special sense that he is the final thought of this time. The history of philosophy, then, is also a system. It forms a system of all these systems of individual philosophers which are separately their own times raised up in thought. As Hegel's *Phenomenology* offers the total progression of all the forms of the experience of consciousness and thus is the science of the experience of consciousness, so his history of philosophy offers the total progression of all the forms of philosophical consciousness understood as a history.

In the three volumes of Hegel's *Lectures on the History of Philosophy*, what today is called the Renaissance is a problem, because in this period one finds no philosophies that in some way can be viewed as system-like. The philosophical thinkers of the Renaissance seem to be part of their times, not summations of it. They seem to be practitioners of rhetoric and of jurisprudence, writers of history and of moral discourses. There are no metaphysical systems in a traditional sense. It is no accident that Cassirer spends so much time on the importance and nature of Nicholas of Cusa as the founding figure of his conception of Renaissance philosophy—he does so because Nicholas has a metaphysics. Why Hegel spends some time discussing Bruno is because Bruno has a cosmology, whereas Pico, Ficino, Pomponazzi, and others do not have, or appear not to have, such potential systematic visions, although Ficino has a multivolume *Platonic Theology*.

The flaw in Hegel's history of philosophy, which set the agenda for all subsequent histories of philosophy—especially the constant division of philosophy into three periods of ancient, medieval, and modern—is the Renaissance, in which conceptual systems of the whole do not arise. Cassirer corrects this account by suggesting that the whole of Renaissance philosophical thought is a system in which all the separate philosophical viewpoints of its figures are parts of a total spirit of the age, which is itself like a system. Although there are no systems such as those authored by a Plato or an Aristotle, an Aquinas or a Kant or a Fichte, there is to some extent a single philosophy authored by multiple figures.

Hegel in his history of philosophy also glosses over the thought of the eighteenth century, which is a second problematic period for his approach. Here again there are no great systems, and Cassirer attempts a correction by working out the total philosophy of the Enlightenment and developing what he calls in the preface to his *Philosophy of the Enlightenment* a "phenomenology of the philosophical spirit."[16] Hegel glosses over the problem of the Enlightenment by selecting for discussion figures who have system-like philosophies such as Leibniz and Hume and making them generally part of modern philosophy.

In his discussion of ancient philosophy Hegel completely avoids the Latins. This is a third problematic period, which affects his treatment of Renaissance humanist philosophy since that period depends so closely on its use of the Latins. As noted earlier, Hegel does not title his first division in the history of philosophy "ancient philosophy"; he titles it "Greek philosophy." The thought of Cicero and the Latins is ignored and is obviously not to be understood as philosophical. Hegel thus began the general exclusion of Latin thought from philosophy that prevails today. He tacitly designates it as essentially rhetorical, poetic, political, historical, and jurisprudential—but not philosophical.

By passing over Latin thought, Hegel establishes an affinity between German philosophy and Greek philosophy—this special relationship that can lead Heidegger to assert that the only spiritual languages are Greek and German. In this way we are led to the commonplace that the Roman and Renaissance thinkers are essentially literary figures and not philosophers because of their absence of concern with metaphysics, with the activity of system-building that is necessary to the German sense of *Wissenschaft*. Once this is done, that mystical union the German philosophers have always felt between their own language and metaphysical productions and the Greeks has been established, to the exclusion of the Latin forms of humanistic and civil thought.

Cassirer's particular achievements in the study of Renaissance thought are great. My point in the foregoing is to suggest the sense in which Cassirer's studies are directed by the Hegelian historiography of philosophy. Cassirer is a coworker in Hegel's fields. Although Cassirer offers a key to the solution of Hegel's problem with the Renaissance, both Cassirer and Hegel miss fully understanding how the Renaissance, or at least Italian Renaissance humanism, offers a unique sense of philosophy by replacing logic with rhetoric. The humanists depart from the claim that only logic is to be studied before other fields because it is required for the study of all else. For the humanists, rhetoric is primary. It is propaedeutic for all other disciplines. It stands side by side with logic as fundamental for philosophical education. The sense in which rhetoric has this fundamental role in thought is what I have attempted to suggest earlier, in the discussion of philosophy and language in chapter 4.

Hegel's Owl and Vico's Road

For Hegel the symbol of the philosophy of history is the flight of the owl. As discussed earlier in a different context in chapter 5, he says, at the end of his preface to the *Philosophy of Right:* "When philosophy paints its grey in grey, then is a shape of life grown old, and with grey in grey it cannot be rejuvenated, but only recognized; the owl of Minerva takes flight only at the falling of the dusk."[17] Philosophy hunts out and knows what has been produced in historical life. But it recognizes things only in a certain way from a certain height. It recognizes only what will fit into the categories of its general scheme such that all it sees must be part of a general progression, each in some way transcended and taken up (*aufgehoben*) in the next.

The symbol for Vico's philosophy is given in his own name, *vico*, in its obsolete meaning designating a little road or lane and also signifying a place, village, or district (Latin *vicus*). James Joyce in *Finnegans Wake* brings this out: "The Vico road goes round and round to meet where terms begin. Still onappealed to by the cycles and unappalled by the recoursers we feel all serene, never you fret, as regards our dutyful cask."[18] The incomplete sentence with which Joyce begins *Finnegans Wake* is a play on Vico's Latin name: "a commodius vicus of recirculation." The flight of Hegel's owl is placeless; it goes out above all that there is. Vico's road is a circle in time; it is the course of beginning, middle, and end that is the experience of any people or nation in history. It is also a place, because any nation has a geography and occupies a place over time in which its phases of life are played out. For Vico there is no total progression, no one cycle in which all nations live. Each nation rises and falls according to the same eternal pattern of ideal, eternal history. Each nation has its own specific birth and end.

Strictly speaking, there are no lectures to be given on "World History" for Vico as there are for Hegel, in which, for example, the Asian cultures are seen to precede the Greek beginnings of Western culture. In Vico's view, the Asian cultures have their own specific histories. There is a story to be told of the life of any nation, and that story will tell of its birth, its heroic moments, and its fall into its own form of barbarism and final end. Because a nation is etymologically a birth (nation, from Latin *nasci*, "to be born") and has a life course, a maturity, and an end, its story philo-sophically understood, that is, understood in its largest and most universal terms, will have structural analogies with the story of any other nation. Humans make the things and the truths of their civil worlds in different, specific ways, but because they are all part of the same humanity they make them according to certain common patterns. The Vichian philosophy of history, Vichian science, is the art of reading this book of the civil world in accordance with these patterns in any nation. In Vico's view, events in history occur neither by the "blind chance" of Epicurus nor by the "deaf neces-sity" of the Stoics. Vico's vision of the structure of history, like Plato's vision of the structure of the universe, is governed by a "pattern set up in the heavens" (*Republic,* 592b).

The art of the philosopher of history is to read this providential pattern in the particular events of the life of any nation, and Vico has given the axioms that guide this art of reading events in his *New Science.* He says that his science is one of meditating and narrating events, and that the proof of it is bound up with the dictum of the Muses (Hesiod, *Theogony,* 36–39) to make the story a tale of what "had, has, and will have to be" (*dovette, deve, dovrà*).[19] The key to Vico's conception of historiography is to practice all the rhetorical arts associated with memory and the making of a speech, the art of topics and the metaphor. For Vico any particular event in history is always a palimpsest; such events are always written over the shadows and traces left by earlier events.

The art of the philosopher of history is to offer a narrative of the subject that relates the causes both natural and moral and the occasions of fortune. Chance events are related against an overall pattern of necessity, and through this combination the providen-tial sense of the course of the nation's life is told. Providence for Vico is unlike that which we have come to understand from other eighteenth-century thinkers, such as Kant in his conception of perpetual peace. Providence is not an overall progress or perfec-tion of events, as Kant understands it. Providence for Vico refers to that overall order or economy of a cycle in which its end is in its beginning and in which the whole cycle is a total prudence, a *prudentia* or *phronēsis* of action, having its own wisdom.

Paul Oskar Kristeller in his essay on "The Moral Thought of Renaissance Humanism" has pointed out that "the humanists shared the view of many ancient and medieval authors that one of the tasks of historiography is to teach a moral lesson."[20] Looked at in broad terms, the Vichian history of the West involves a first *corso*, or course, in which there is an age of gods (an age in which the whole of human experience was organized in terms of a pantheon of gods) and an age of heroes (an age in which all human institutions were ordered in terms of the virtues embodied in the personae of heroes). Homer is the end of this original heroic age, and Homer's poems are the summary statement of this lost world of gods and heroes. After Homer begins the third age of humans, in which the memories of the gods dim and the virtues, which were actual character traits of the heroes, become moral concepts and principles that can be intellectually expressed. In this third age philosophy is born, and myth gives way to metaphysics. The pursuit of self-knowledge of Socrates, the systems of Plato and Aristotle, the schools of the Epicureans, Stoics, and Skeptics and their Latin embodiments all develop in the third age of the intellect. With the fall of the Greco-Roman world, the ideal eternal history of the *corso* of the ancient world of Western culture comes to an end.

Upon the ruins of this ancient world arise the analogous three ages of the *ricorso*, or recourse. The *ricorso* has its origins in a return to religion and to the original customs of religious rites, marriage, and burial involved in the spread of Christendom. This religious age is succeeded by the feudal period of heroic activity, of medieval courts and crusades. In this *ricorso*, the activity of the ages of gods and of heroes that culminates in the society and thought of the medieval world is summarized by Dante. Vico calls Dante the "Tuscan Homer."[21] Dante stands to this *ricorso* as Homer stands to the original *corso* of the West. And, like Homer, Dante ushers in a third age of humanistic thought and philosophy. The Renaissance begins the modern age of secular thought. Renaissance philosophy is created from a revival of the corresponding thought of the first *corso*, the thought of Socrates, Plato, Aristotle, and the ancient schools. The *ricorso* is not just another *corso* because the memory of much of the first remains in various ways in the *ricorso*. The *ricorso* is built upon the old *corso* like a new city is built upon an old one, a new polis upon an earlier one, the evidences of which are often showing through but are only dimly apprehended.

It is not until the point of the Renaissance that what was there at the end of the former *corso* is consciously reappropriated and made the theme of the new, modern world of the third age of the *ricorso*. Vico regards the thought of the Middle Ages as essentially tied to religion, to theology. This reappropriation is the way the world of the ancients gains touch with the new world of the moderns. The *ricorso* of any nation's life is not a Hegelian *Aufhebung* ("supersession") of its past. Although a *ricorso* involves a memory of elements of the earlier *corso*, and in this sense "takes up" the *corso* in itself, the *ricorso* is not a progressive development of the *corso*. The *ricorso* does not represent an "advance" on the *corso*. It does not move the life of the nation closer to the realization of an overall telos, or absolute state. The *ricorso*, although built upon the *corso*, meets an analogous end in its own final barbarism. No age is a golden age or an age in which human good is finally realized. Vico looks at history and never smiles.

From the Renaissance develops the full barbarism of the modern world of the West, with its overly rationalistic forms of thought—the barbarism of reflection (*la barbarie della riflessione*), which Vico says is more barbaric than the crude barbarism of sense (*la barbarie del senso*) of the first age of any *corso*, which he says is an honest barbarism.[22] In this third age, that in which Vico finds himself and in which we also find ourselves, the creations of human imagination (*fantasia*) dim and the gods and heroes are forgotten. Clear and distinct ideas reign and language is used to flatter and confound; a false wit governs human activity, which pursues ever more ingenious forms of life, and thought becomes ever more abstract, until finally we reach what Elio Gianturco, one of Vico's translators, has called a Cartesian world, "a world of scientific research, technology, and gadgets, which invade and condition our lives."[23] This, then, is a moral tale which Vico tells in the spirit of the historiography of the humanists. Vico's *New Science* is a moral discourse. It is not a history in the later, modern sense.

Prudential Wisdom

The moral discourse of the *New Science* is constructed by the revival of those ways of thinking which are imbedded in the thought of the Renaissance Italian humanists. There is a close connection between rhetoric and historiography in Renaissance humanism. Kristeller points out: "We may dislike the style of the humanists, but their literary ambitions do not stand in the way of their critical judgment or their use of historical evidence any more than is the case with ancient or modern historians."[24]

Vico claims to found his metaphysics of history on a "new critical art" (*una nuova arte critica*). He achieves this historical speech in which the mentality of the Renaissance is central by the revival of those forms of thinking, those canons of thought which Descartes deliberately excludes from his principles for the conduct of right reasoning in the sciences, as discussed earlier in chapter 4. Vico goes back to the Latins and reads the Greeks through the Latins. One of his heroes is Cicero, and in his tale of Western culture in terms of *corso* and *ricorso*, Vico's aim is to reestablish the Ciceronian and humanist interconnection between prudence, wisdom, and eloquence (*prudentia, sapientia,* and *eloquentia*). Eloquence is wisdom speaking and prudence is wisdom acting.

When in his history Hegel considers Cicero directly, not just the Renaissance revival of Ciceronian philosophy, as mentioned earlier, he remarks that philosophy must be distinguished from popular philosophy. He says that the writings of Cicero can be

categorized in this way. Cicero commands a kind of philosophizing that has its place and in which admirable things are said.
But Hegel claims such thinking is not truly philosophical. In this
way Hegel is the inheritor of Descartes' spirit of right reasoning—
the tying of philosophy to logic.

In the view of Vichian philosophy, the Renaissance has both
a day side and a night side. It has a night side because it is the
beginning of the end. It begins the last stage of a *corso;* philosophy
brings about the reality of the "intelligible universal" (*universale
intelligibile*) and establishes the seeming perfection of the intelligible. When the philosophers arrive in history, the mythic thought
of the poets is about to perish or to lie permanently etherized upon
the table. The logic of Vico's "imaginative universals" (*universali
fantastici*) of the ages of gods and heroes, the form of the original
mythico-poetic mind of humanity, is lost.[25] Yet there is a day side,
because when philosophy is properly joined with rhetoric, poetics,
and history it offers the possibility to speak against the barbarity of
the modern age. When philosophy remembers its natural connections with eloquence, it offers the only possibility for wisdom and
prudence or moral discourse that can be found in the world of
science, technology, and gadgets that invade and condition our
lives. In this world, the speech of the Vichian thinker is almost
naturally misunderstood, if it is ever heard at all. All too often the
humanist philosopher is in the position of Ovid as he exclaims, in
his exile in Tomis: "Here I am the barbarian because no one understands me" (*Tristia,* 5.10.37). With this exclamation Rousseau
begins his *First Discourse.*

Vico claimed that the proof of his science is for the reader to
tell the story of history to himself as the story of what had, has,
and will have to be. This great art of memory, when practiced on
history, shows that the circle is the ultimate metaphysical unit of
human experience and that this circular grasp of events is the ultimate guide to human conduct. To think from the perspective of
the circle is always to think in terms of origins and revivals. In the
Physics Aristotle says that perfect motion is in the circle and that

circular motion is the measure of all motion. He says: "This also explains the common saying that human affairs form a circle, and that there is a circle in all other things that have a natural movement and coming into being and passing away. This is because all other things are discriminated by time, and end and begin as though conforming to a cycle; for even time itself is thought to be a circle" (223b25–30).

Conclusion

We are left with the converse of the earlier images of Hegel and Vico—now we have Hegel's road and Vico's owl. In the *Phenomenology of Spirit*, the whole progression of the shapes of the experience of consciousness is a "highway of despair" (*Weg der Verzweiflung*). Hegel's road is a single road, the turning points of which are in no way the realization of absolute knowing. Absolute knowing is possible only of the whole. Only at the completion of the whole course is the despair of incomplete thinking relieved. Hegel says that his system as a whole is a circle, and in the *Science of Logic* he adds that it is in fact a circle of circles, a kind of circle made up of links like a chain, formed into a circle. But it is a single circle, even though composed of smaller circles. It is a one-time perfect motion in which beginning is brought into contact with end. All recourses are transcended yet preserved (*aufgehoben*) within the single course. In this the Renaissance can occupy very little place at all. This is so because the very sense of Renaissance humanist philosophy, with its connection to rhetoric, topics, and imagination, does not allow for the sense of system that Hegelian thought requires to count as real philosophy, real *Wissenschaft*. The culmination of the ancient world in the Latins is missed by Hegel—and thus the Renaissance is essentially missed. Hegel has no way, no historiographical perspective from which to really speak about the Renaissance except in negative or tentative terms.

Vico, in his last public address, his remarks to the Academy of Oziosi, said: "I hold the opinion that if eloquence does not regain the luster of the Latins and Greeks in our time, when our sciences will have made progress equal to and perhaps even greater than theirs, it will be because the sciences are taught completely stripped of every badge of eloquence."[26] In Vico's view of history, the Renaissance philosophy of humanism based on rhetorical and poetic conceptions of language becomes the crucial middle term through which we can join ourselves with the heroic mind of the ancients. Modern philosophy, in Vico's history, is a second and even more severe descent into the inferno of the purely reflective intellect, a descent without the prudence of Odysseus, without the guidance of Virgil, and without the divine concern of Beatrice.

Vichian philosophy becomes a way for the individual to live in a barbaric age. It is a medicine to avert barbarism in the individual, but it is not a cure for the processes of history through which the age moves into that ultimate civil disease of reflective life. Vico is Hegel's owl of Minerva (the goddess of wisdom) who, as the embodiment of philosophical thought, takes flight only at the dusk, to bring together the events of the day. Vico in this sense is the closing figure of the rhetorically based philosophy of humanism. But Vico is also Minerva in the sense of the armed Minerva, Bellona, the goddess of warfare and civil order. Vico as the double Minerva imitates the figure of rhetoric herself, as described in a poem dedicated to the sixteenth-century historian of Rome, Carlo Sigonio: "One hand is open, the other carries a spear."[27] Vico is at war with the Cartesian world that, through technology and reflection, would deprive us of the civil wisdom of humanism. In the end, the image of the owl of Minerva is insufficient to convey Vico's position, for, as Andrea Battistini has claimed, Vico is also "a philosopher of the dawn, interested in the first appearance of the light; he is looking not for the owl of Minerva, but for the skylark, the herald of the morning, as Shakespeare says."[28] As the practitioner of rhetorical inquiry, Vico uses rhetoric and poetics as his means to take us back to the origin, to the place where logic cannot go, to the dawn of the human world.

Vico and Hegel are two examples of thinkers whose philosophies of history lead to philosophies of the history of philosophy. For both the history of philosophy is constructed backward, toward the origin. In this way we as moderns acquire a memory of how philosophy has come to us, and a background against which new ideas can occur. The crucial issue is how the ancients are placed in relation to the moderns. For Vico there is no continuous line back to the ancients. Our access to the ancients is through the Renaissance. Renaissance philosophy is formed in terms of a revival of the ancients. There is no continuous process of thought from the ancients to the modern world. We can proceed back through the Renaissance humanist tradition, first to the Latins and then to the Greeks. The humanist reading of the Greeks revives the interpretation of their thought through attention to its interpretation by the Latin authors. By contrast, modern philosophy in the hands of Descartes is a break with the humanist conception of philosophy that connects philosophy with rhetoric and poetic. Additionally, in Vico's view medieval philosophy is theology, and is important only to the extent that some aspects of it are taken up into the beginning of the Renaissance.

In Hegel's view, there is a continuous line of philosophical thought that can be traced from the moderns back through the Middle Ages to the ancients. In this view, Greek philosophy can be confronted directly by a continuous reconstruction of the past. The problems and systems of Greek philosophy can be exposited, and it can be shown how philosophy itself moves forward from them through the systems of the Middle Ages to the dawn of modern philosophy in the rationalists and the empiricists. This tripartite division of Greek, medieval, and modern is the scheme of the history of philosophy most familiar to us and is the basis of most courses in the history of philosophy. But, as attention to Vico's philosophy shows, it passes quickly over the Latins and the Renaissance, granting them little intrinsic value.

Philosophical Practics

7

PHILOSOPHICAL WRITING

The reader of the history of philosophy may be led to contribute to the scholarship on particular problems or figures within it. Should this occur there are better and worse ways to present one's thoughts. In the discussion of the principles of philosophical writing that follows, I intend to say not what is required for the production of original philosophies, but what is required for the interpretation of such philosophies. This interpretation may take either critical or speculative form, as described in chapter 1. Since the ancients, the principles of composition have been known. As Quintilian states them, in regard to writing, they are *inventio*, the discovery and compilation of materials; *dispositio*, their structure and arrangement; and *elocutio*, their formulation in language (*Institutio Oratoria*, 3.3). These are principles that any writer follows naturally in the production of a work, but deliberate attention to these principles provides a guide to good writing.

Inventio, in modern terms, is the research the author does in order to write on a subject. In philosophy this usually takes the form of reading what has been written on the subject and meditating on the themes, arguments, and problems involved. This process may also include conversations with others. The ways of researching a specific subject are beyond the scope of these remarks. What research is needed and how it is to be done is determined largely by the nature of the topic on which the author plans to write. When the author is prepared to write on a subject, to advance a particular argument or interpretation, how is it to be formulated?

My aim in what follows is simply practical advice. I wish to suggest *one* model for writing a philosophical essay. It is a model especially well suited to essays on figures or topics in the history of philosophy. It is distilled from four decades of writing, editing, and refereeing work for publication, including time I have spent as a journal editor. I have taught this model for many years to students in my graduate seminars who were preparing themselves for careers in professional philosophy and who have repeatedly demonstrated the ability to employ it in writings that they have had accepted for publication. Thus I have a great deal of confidence in it. But I do not mean that it is the only model for a good philosophical essay or paper. It is the one I use and teach. Practice at writing a piece according to this format might be likened to practice at life-drawing in art. Once drawing the human form is mastered, the artist is free to modify the form's elements and produce variations. But the variations are not projections in thin air; they are done against the prior grasp of a definite structure. A similar analogy could be made in relation to learning music and composition.

We may add to Quintilian's statement of principles Horace's dictum that "right thinking is the first principle and source of writing," so that "when the subject is well conceived, words will follow on spontaneously" (*Ars Poetica*, 309–11). The author must emerge from research on a subject with a well-conceived thesis. Without such a thesis to guide it, the writing will be weak and lack authority. Writing, as is well known, is an act of discovery. The author can expect that a well-conceived thesis or argument may alter in the course of being put into words. The three classical principles of composition enumerated earlier are not independent elements. They are dialectically interrelated such that, in inquiring into a subject, the author is at the same time organizing the research in terms of a potential thesis and beginning to sense how to write the essay. In writing the essay, the author may revise the thesis or encounter the need to discover further dimensions of the subject and bring other, unexpected materials into play. Nothing is complete until the essay is complete and forms a whole.

Structure of the Essay

Writing is an art that comes more naturally to some than others. The basis of good writing is good reading. The most one can offer are tips and clues to be considered in writing a philosophical piece. The following model is composed solely of such tips and clues.

1. *Title.* The title needs to let the reader know as clearly and immediately as possible what the essay is about. It does not need to capture fully the particular thesis or argument of the essay, but the informed reader should be able instantly to grasp its subject. The title might involve an interesting combination of words or juxtaposition of ideas, but it should not be simply poetic or imagistic, making the subject of the essay a mystery to the potential reader. In short, the informed reader should be able to sense some context for the essay from its title, a context that will quickly become clear as the reader begins to read it.

2. *First page.* The first page or paragraphs of an essay stand to the rest of the essay the way a preface or an introduction stands to the chapters of a book. The reader should learn from the start why it has been written. The author faces here the question of audience and needs to establish a rapport with the reader. The author can do this by concisely characterizing for the reader the prevailing views on the subject. Ideally, the essay begins by calling forth something about the subject that the informed reader will easily recognize, with the purpose of claiming that there is something problematic about the current understanding of the subject. In this opening, the author introduces the original point of the essay by placing it against what has commonly been thought about the subject.

3. *Thesis paragraph*. This "first page" or sequence of introductory paragraphs should lead up to a single paragraph, or part of a paragraph, in which the original thesis of the essay is fully stated. This statement may be done in two ways, of which I much prefer the second. One way is to explain in a few sentences what the essay intends to prove and to give the reader some indication of how the author intends to proceed with this proof in what is to come. Another way is to indicate the thesis in terms of a question or several interrelated questions, but not a long list of questions. The rest of the essay, then, is the development of the answers to these questions, one by one. The first way, that of stating a claim to be proved, might be seen as "Cartesian" in temperament. The second way, that of setting the thesis up in questions, might be seen as "Socratic." The question, in philosophical thought, is rhetorically very powerful; it draws the reader in and arouses curiosity as to what the author considers to be an answer. The statement of a claim and its alleged proof rhetorically make the reader a potential opponent from the start, with the author defending the case. By contrast, the question keeps open a sense of inquiry and asks the reader to participate, even if, in the end, the reader may not agree. The claim-proof approach is akin to what is known in classical logic as the *ars critica;* the question-and-answer approach is more akin to the *ars topica* (as discussed earlier in chapter 4).

4. *Body*. Every good essay should have a beginning, middle, and end. The foregoing has established the beginning. The body of the essay, the bulk of its pages, is the middle. Here, in a progressive fashion, the proof and evidence for the claim or claims of the author are reached or the answers to the question are developed, with one leading to another.

a. In moving from one main point to another, the author should always bring the reader along. Restate in a sentence what has been claimed or established thus far before moving on to the next point.

b. If, in writing the body of the essay, the author comes to an impasse, a way out is to put the nature of the impasse into a question and move on from it as a new starting point.

c. Avoid long quotations. Quote only a phrase or a sentence containing the crucial words of the point at issue. The author should restate briefly what otherwise would appear in a lengthy quotation. Nothing is usually gained by having long quotations break up the flow of the text. A good rule is not to quote more than what can easily be run into the text without needing to be set off. Few realize that, in fact, any quotation of less than 100 words can be run into the text, according to various style manuals. If a long, set-off quotation is used, the author must be convinced that it is truly necessary, and what appears in it should be fully discussed.

d. In criticizing another thinker's view or interpreting part of another thinker's work, do not engage in lengthy exposition, re-creating the details of the whole line of thought in question. Precisely state the point in question and summarize it only to the extent necessary to confront clearly and fairly the other's standpoint.

5. *Length.* A good length for an essay is about twenty double-spaced, typed pages, or about 5,000 words of text. Usually, if a scholarly essay is much longer than this, the topic should have been more closely limited. Almost anything that can be said in thirty or forty pages can be said in twenty or so pages.

6. *Footnotes.* a. Avoid extensive documentation unless the nature of the subject truly requires it. It is always possible to multiply footnotes and documentation. More difficult is to strike a balance and supply a proper amount of footnotes that the reader can find useful and to the point.

b. Avoid explanatory footnotes. What appears in most explanatory footnotes can either be omitted or incorporated into the text. An explanatory footnote needs to appear to the reader as necessary, even though not central to the essay's thesis, and not just inserted as an additional comment. Especially to be avoided is a series of footnotes that undergird a text so that the author seems to have become a commentator on his or her own work.

7. *Final paragraph.* An essay should be so presented that a reader familiar with the subject discussed can read the first and last

paragraphs of the essay and grasp what the author is maintaining. The body or middle of the piece contains the evidence, details, examples, interpretations, and particular arguments that support what the author claims. The last paragraph literally can begin with "In conclusion" or "In summary." In it the author restates and draws together what has been claimed in the body of the work. To the author this paragraph may seem redundant or unnecessary, because what has been said before seems clear to the author. But the reader needs to know, finally, from the author what has been intended. This ending is also an opportunity for the author to modify in any sense the general nature of the thesis or to stress points which must not be misunderstood. If possible, the author may close the essay with one good, inspired sentence that brings the issue home to the reader.

One ending that should be avoided is the claim by the author that this essay has cleared the ground so that the important issues involved in the subject can be treated in the future. An essay of this form, leading to such a conclusion, is ordinarily useless and of little interest. Such an approach is weak and puts off the issues of real interest to another time. The author should strive to address an important issue squarely and say something about it, not to clear the way, supposedly, for a more substantive treatment.

Philosophical Style

Aristotle begins the *Rhetoric* with the assertion that "rhetoric is the counterpart of dialectic" (1354a1). Philosophical thought must always stand the test of logical reasoning in its widest sense, but in communicating ideas the philosophical writer has rhetoric and its principles as a counterpart. The foregoing model of a philosophical essay primarily relates to the second principle of composition mentioned earlier: how thought on a subject is structured. The third principle concerns how a subject is expressed. There are certainly better and worse ways to express ideas in language, and simply having this point constantly in mind is useful while writing a philosophical essay. A philosophical writer shares this kind of self-awareness with other types of writers. It is common knowledge that much of what one encounters in philosophical literature could be improved. This does not mean that philosophical writing should be simplistic; it means only that it should be good writing on difficult subjects.

It is a great asset to develop a good writing style early. There is no formula for good writing, but the following are several considerations.

1. *Imitation.* As with any art, acquisition of the art of good philosophical writing begins in imitation. It is most helpful to select a figure whose work can serve as an example to follow. This is a personal choice. I have been most impressed with the command of English in the writings of R. G. Collingwood. In addition to his mastery of philosophical prose in English, his book *An Essay on Philosophical Method* is useful for anyone interested in writing, especially the final chapter, "Philosophy as a Branch of Literature." (See also my remarks in chapter 4.) Also worth mentioning in this connection is Brand Blanshard's little book *On Philosophical Style.* Blanshard, too, was a master of philosophical English. Bertrand Russell and A. N. Whitehead are also good philosophical writers, whether or not one agrees with their philosophies. At the height of the ordinary-language philosophy movement, J. L. Austin was much admired for the style of his essays. Henri Bergson wrote in an excellent manner, but to use his work as a model would pose special problems of transference from French to English. In the American tradition, William James is much admired. James said he often worked all day and at its end had produced only one good sentence. By imitation as a principle of good writing I do not mean simple copying or aping. I have in mind a model from which to learn, transpose, and adopt.

2. *Editing.* In a purely practical sense, any writer can benefit from editing for style, grammar, and spelling. If it is possible to find a knowledgable person who can read one's work from this

perspective, the work will always be improved. If such an arrangement is not possible, the author can consider first gaining some intellectual and temporal distance from the work and then going back through it to edit.

3. *Checking.* When the essay is in final form, the author should check the information in each footnote and the wording of each quotation against the original works. No matter how careful the author is in writing and revising, it is very likely that a page number or publication date in a footnote is in error, or that a word or two is omitted from some quotations. There is no reason not to have such information completely accurate.

4. *Reading aloud.* In arriving at the final version of any work, it is most useful to read the text aloud. It need not be read to another person, although this is helpful. The author can read it aloud alone. In so doing the author will immediately discover expressions or sentences that do not flow well or that need transition and amplification. Infelicities missed or tolerated on the page by the eye are easily caught by the ear.

5. *Tendency to qualify.* The single worst tendency of authors of philosophical writing is continually to qualify or modify what is said. It is natural to think that if one says something tentatively one will preempt criticism. Thus an author writes "It appears that such and such is the case" when the author really is claiming that "such and such" is actually the case. The author will not in fact avoid the critic with such locutions. The claim should be stated directly, without a rhetorical attempt to hedge what is said. Any philosophical work gains in authority for the reader when the author says what is meant in no uncertain terms. If there are logical disclaimers or modifications to be attached to a claim, these should be stated clearly and forcefully. Nothing is lost and everything is gained by revising a text so that it has a good declarative style.

6. *Paragraphing.* Any text is also improved by good paragraphing. A good rule, in working over a text, is to see that there is *at least* one paragraph break on every typed page. The reader is carried along by thought that falls into units and that does not

wind on from one thing to the next. A work is often improved by dividing it into parts, with subtitles for each. These allow the reader a natural overview and give each part of the subject treated a definite place.

The model for a philosophical essay that I have suggested is one that many have used successfully, and once mastered it provides for variations. In beginning to write such a piece, it is better to have some model in mind than to just start writing in the hope that a structure will emerge. There is no formula to produce good writing, but an author cannot go wrong by giving attention to the several suggestions above, especially the selection of a philosopher whose command of language is exemplary. Often attention to the simplest and most obvious principles has a great effect on how something is expressed. The author gains a great satisfaction, not only in conveying ideas, but in conveying them well.

8

PHILOSOPHICAL LITERACY

In 1987 E. D. Hirsch Jr. published *Cultural Literacy: What Every American Needs to Know,* which became a best seller. In addition to essays on cultural literacy, Hirsch's work contains an appendix of 5,000 essential names, phrases, dates, and concepts by which the reader's cultural literacy can be tested. I came to the idea for the following list when reading Hirsch's general list.

Any one respondent may know more than another about a particular term or name on the list. A response to the item "pragmatism," for example, need not entail the knowledge that the term was likely first used by C. S. Peirce in a paper to the Metaphysical Club in Cambridge (Mass.) in the 1870s and that its meaning was a matter of argument between Peirce and William James. "Pragmatism" should invoke at least some statement in the reader's mind of one of its major tenets and its identification with the work of some of its major representatives. The "square of opposition" might call to mind the traditional square of opposition as well as the problems it involves in regard to the principle of existential import. *Philia* may call to mind its meaning of love as friendship, but also its etymological connection to *philo-* as used by Pythagoras in the traditional account of the coining of the terms *philosopher* and *philosophy.*

157

"Shaftesbury" may call to mind the author of the *Characteristics* associated with the Cambridge Platonists, and perhaps further, his project in the unfinished *Second Characters* of a scheme of morals based on the study of emblems. "Performative utterance" may call forth J. L. Austin's distinction between performative and constative utterances, such that "I promise" accomplishes the act of promising, as opposed to "he promised" that only reports one. "Family resemblance" might call forth Ludwig Wittgenstein's assertion in *Philosophical Investigations* that concept words do not denote clearly determined concepts but mark family resemblances between things that the concept labels; that there need be no common property possessed by all the things defined in the same way.

One needs to have some specific and immediate formulation of what an item is in order to recognize it intellectually. As with Hirsch's list, there is no requirement that one's knowledge of what an item means must have been acquired by firsthand study or acquaintance. One's recognition may depend on secondary sources, study guides, handbooks, conversation, mention in lectures, and so on. The principle of literacy is that these terms can be employed in the course of philosophical discussion and conversation without the presumption that they require special explanation or identification.

Any list of this kind is provisional and subject to revision, but it supplies a standard where otherwise there is none. It is likely that no reader will know well all the items on the list, but anyone who has completed a full study of philosophy may know nearly all of the entries to some extent. The items on the list have been selected from reference works such as *The Cambridge Dictionary of Philosophy*, *The Encyclopedia of Philosophy*, the glossaries in the volumes of the *Routledge History of Philosophy*, and from smaller dictionaries of philosophy by various authors. The list contains 700 items.

The List

abduction

Peter Abelard

Absolute

accident

a fortiori

agape

agathon

alchemy

Jean Le Rond d'Alembert

Samuel Alexander

Alexandrian school

Saint Ambrose

analytic philosophy

analytic-synthetic distinction

anamnesis

Anaxagoras

Anaximander

Anaximenes

angst

Saint Anselm

antinomy

Antisthenes

Apollonian spirit

aporia

a posteriori knowledge

a priori knowledge

Saint Thomas Aquinas

archē

aretē

argument from analogy

argumentum ad hominem

argumentum ad ignorantium

argumentum ad misericordiam

argumentum ad populum

argumentum ad verecundiam

Aristotle

Antoine Arnauld

artificial intelligence

asceticism

atomism

ataraxia

Saint Augustine

J. L. Austin

Averroes

Avicenna

axiology

axiomatic method

A. J. Ayer

Francis Bacon

Roger Bacon

bad faith

Karl Barth

Pierre Bayle

behaviorism

being

Being and Nothingness

Being and Time

Jeremy Bentham

Nicolas Berdyaev

Henri Bergson

George Berkeley

biconditional

bioethics

Jakob Boehme

Boethius

Saint Bonaventure

Boolean algebra

borderline case

Bernard Bosanquet

Robert Boyle

bracketing

F. H. Bradley

Franz Brentano

C. D. Broad

Giordano Bruno

Martin Buber

Jean Buridan

Edmund Burke

Joseph Butler

Cabala

John Calvin

Cambridge Platonists

Tommaso Campanella

Georg Cantor

cardinal virtues

Rudolf Carnap

Cartesian dualism

Ernst Cassirer

categorical imperative

categorical syllogism

category

category mistake

catharsis

causal law

cause, proximate and remote

Cicero

cogito ergo sum

cognitive science

coherence theory of truth

R. G. Collingwood

communitarianism

complementary class

Comte's law of three stages

conatus

The Concept of Mind

conceptualism

Étienne Bonnot de Condillac

conditional proof

conditio sine qua non

Marquis de Condorcet

Confessions

consciousness

Consolation of Philosophy

constructive dilemma

contextualism

continental philosophy

contractarianism

contraposition

contraries

converse

Copernican revolution

copula

Corpus Iuris Civilis (*Digest of Justinian*)

correspondence theory of truth

cosmological argument

Counter-Enlightenment

counterfactuals

Victor Cousin

covering law model

Cratylus

creation ex nihilo

Creative Evolution

critical realism

critical theory

Crito

Benedetto Croce

crucial experiment

cybernetics

Cynics

Cyrenaics

Darwinism

Dasein

De Anima

decision theory

deconstruction

deduction

definiendum

definiens

definite description

deism

demiurge

Democritus

De Morgan's laws

denotation

De Officiis

deontological ethics

De Rerum Natura

Jacques Derrida

René Descartes

determinism

John Dewey

dialectic

dialectical materialism

dianoia

Denis Diderot

différance

dilemma

Wilhelm Dilthey

Ding an sich

Diogenes Laertius

Diogenes the Cynic

Dionysian spirit

Discourse on Method

disjunctive proposition

distribution

dogmatism

double negation

doxa

Duns Scotus

Meister Eckhart

eclecticism

The Economic and Philosophical Manuscripts

Jonathan Edwards

efficient cause

eidos

élan vital

Eleatic school

elenchus

Ralph Waldo Emerson

emotive theory of ethics

Empedocles

empiricism

Encyclopédie

Friedrich Engels

Enlightenment

Enneads

en soi

entelechy

enthymeme

Epictetus

Epicureanism

epistemology

Desiderius Erasmus

John Scotus Erigena

eros

eschatology

An Essay Concerning Human Understanding

An Essay on Philosophical Method

esse est percipi

The Essence of Christianity

essentialism

eternal return

ethical intuitionism

ethical naturalism

ethical objectivism

ethical relativism

ethical subjectivism

ethos

Eudemian Ethics

eudaimonia

Euler diagram

evil, problem of

existential generalization

existential import

existentialism

Experience and Nature

expression theory of art

The Expulsion of the Triumphant Beast

The Fable of the Bees

fact-value distinction

faculty psychology

fallacy of accent

fallacy of accident

fallacy of division

fallacy of equivocation

fallacy of four terms

fallacy of misplaced concreteness

fallacy of simple location

fallibilism

family resemblance

Ludwig Feuerbach

J. G. Fichte

Marsilio Ficino

field theory

final cause

First and *Second Discourses*

first *Critique*

first-order logic

first philosophy

formal cause

Michel Foucault

foundationalism

Frankfurt School

free will problem

Gottlieb Frege

functionalism

Hans-Georg Gadamer

Galen

Galileo

game theory

Pierre Gassendi

Geist

Geisteswissenschaften

Gemeinschaft

general systems theory

genetic epistemology

genetic fallacy

gestalt

Étienne Gilson

given

Gnosticism

Gödel's incompleteness theorem

Nelson Goodman

Baltasar Gracián

great chain of being

Greek Academy

T. H. Green

Robert Grosseteste

Hugo Grotius

The Guide of the Perplexed

Jürgen Habermas

haecceity

Johann Georg Hamann

Nicolai Hartmann

hedonism

hedonistic calculus

G. W. F. Hegel

Martin Heidegger

Heisenberg indeterminacy
   principle

Hellenistic philosophy

Helvétius

Heraclides of Pontus

Heraclitus

J. G. von Herder

hermeneutic circle

hermeneutics

hermeneutics of suspicion

hermetism

historical determinism

historicism

Thomas Hobbes

Baron d'Holbach

Friedrich Hölderlin

How to Do Things with Words

Wilhelm von Humboldt

David Hume

Edmund Husserl

hylē

Hypatia

hypothetical syllogism

hypothetico-deductive method

idealism

clear and distinct ideas

identity of indiscernibles

idols of the cave

idols of the marketplace

idols of the theater

idols of the tribe

ignoratio elenchi

illicit process of the major term

immanence

indeterminacy of translation

indexical expressions

induction

induction by simple
    enumeration

infinite regress argument

informal fallacy

innate ideas

*An Inquiry into Meaning and
    Truth*

instrumentalism

intentionality

Ion

Ionian philosophy

Isocrates

is-ought distinction

I-Thou relationship

Friedrich Jacobi

William James

Karl Jaspers

C. G. Jung

just war theory

Immanuel Kant

Johannes Kepler

Søren Kierkegaard

Heinrich von Kleist

knowledge by acquaintance and
    knowledge by description

Jacques Lacan

Julien Offray de La Mettrie

Susanne Langer

language game

laws of thought

Lebensphilosophie

legal positivism

legal realism

Gottfried Wilhelm Leibniz

V. I. Lenin

Gotthold Ephraim Lessing

Leucippus

Leviathan

Emmanuel Levinas

C. I. Lewis

liar paradox

life-world

light of nature

linguistic philosophy

John Locke

logical atomism

logical positivism

Logical Syntax of Language

logos

Longinus

Lucretius

Georg Lukacs

Martin Luther

Lyceum

Jean-François Lyotard

Ernst Mach

Machiavelli

macrocosm, microcosm

Maimonides

major premise

Nicolas Malebranche

Man a Machine

Manichaeanism

Marcus Aurelius

Jacques Maritain

Karl Marx

Marxism

material cause

materialism

George Herbert Mead

Meditations on First Philosophy

Alexius Meinong

Moses Mendelssohn

Meno

Maurice Merleau-Ponty

metaethics

metalanguage

metaphilosophy

metaphysical realism

method of agreement

method of agreement and
    difference, joint

method of concomitant variation

method of difference

method of residues

middle Platonism

middle Stoicism

middle term

Milesians

James Mill

John Stuart Mill

mimetic theory of art

minor premise

modal logic

modus ponens

modus tollens

monad

Monadology

monism

Michel de Montaigne

Baron de Montesquieu

G. E. Moore

Thomas More

myth of Er

myth of the cave

naive realism

naturalistic fallacy

natural kind

natural law

natural religion

natura naturans

natura naturata

necessary and contingent truth

necessary condition

neo-Kantianism

Neoplatonism

neo-scholasticism

New England transcendentalists

New Organon

new realism

The New Science

Isaac Newton

Nicholas of Cusa

Nicomachean Ethics

Friedrich Nietzsche

nihilism

noetic

nominalism

non causa pro causa

non-Euclidean geometry

nous

Novalis

obversion

occasionalism

William of Ockham

Ockham's razor

Of Grammatology

Of Learned Ignorance

On Liberty

"On Sense and Reference"

*On the Aesthetic Education of
Man in a Series of Letters*

On the Genealogy of Morality

ontological argument

ontological difference

operationalism

"Oration on the Dignity of
Man"

The Order of Things

ordinary-language philosophy

Origen

José Ortega y Gasset

ostensive definition

other minds problem

ousia

panentheism

panpsychism

pantheism

Paracelsus

paradigm case argument

paradox

Parmenides

Pascal's wager

The Passions of the Soul

patristic authors

Peano postulates

Charles Sanders Peirce

performative utterance

Peripatetic school

personal identity

personalism

Peter Lombard

petitio principii

Phaedo

Phaedrus

phenomenalism

phenomenological reduction

phenomenology

Phenomenology of Spirit

philia

Philo Judaeus

Les philosophes

philosophical anthropology

philosophy of mind

Philosophy of Right

The Philosophy of Symbolic Forms

phronēsis

physis

Pico della Mirandola

picture theory of meaning

Plato

Platonic Academy of Florence

Plotinus

pluralism

Poetics

poiēsis

polis

Karl Popper

Porphyry

Port-Royal Logic

possible worlds

Posterior Analytics

post hoc, ergo propter hoc

postmodern

post-structuralism

potency

pragmatic contradiction

pragmatic theory of truth

pragmatism

The Praise of Folly

praxis

predicate logic

preestablished harmony

pre-Socratics

prime matter

prime mover

The Prince

Principia Ethica

principle of contradiction

principle of sufficient reason

Principles of Psychology

Prior Analytics

private language argument

privileged access

Process and Reality

process philosophy

propositional-predicate calculus

Proslogion

Protagoras

protocol statement

Pyrrhonism

Pythagoras

qualities, primary and secondary

quantification theory

quiddity

W. V. O. Quine

quod erat demonstrandum
  (Q.E.D.)

Petrus Ramus

ratio

rationalism

John Rawls

real definition

realism

reductio ad absurdum

Thomas Reid

relations, internal and external

relativism

Renaissance humanism

res cogitans

res extensa

Jean-Jacques Rousseau

Josiah Royce

Bertrand Russell

Gilbert Ryle

George Santayana

Jean-Paul Sartre

Scepticism and Animal Faith

Max Scheler

F. W. J. von Schelling

Friedrich Schiller

Friedrich Schleiermacher

Scholasticism

Arthur Schopenhauer

Science of Logic

scientific realism

Scottish common sense
  philosophy

second *Critique*

self-evidence

Seneca

sensationalism

sense-data

sensus communis

set theory

Seventh Letter

Sextus Empiricus

Shaftesbury

situation ethics

Skepticism

slave morality

slippery slope argument

Adam Smith

social contract

Socrates

Socratic irony

Socratic method

solipsism

Vladimir Solovyov

sophia

Sophist

Sophistical Refutations

Sophists

sōphrosynē

sorites

sound argument

speculative philosophy

speech act theory

Herbert Spencer

Benedict de Spinoza

square of opposition

state of nature

stipulative definition

Stoicism

P. F. Strawson

structuralism

Francisco Suárez

subject-object dichotomy

sublime

sub specie aeternitatis

substance

substance, primary and
secondary

substratum

sufficient condition

sui generis

Summa Contra Gentiles

Summa Theologiae

summum bonum

Swedenborgianism

Symposium

synthetic a priori

systems theory

tabula rasa

tautology

technē

teleological argument

teleology

tertiary qualities

Tertullian

Thales of Miletus

Theatetus

theodicy

Theophrastus

A Theory of Justice

theosophy

third *Critique*

Timaeus

third man argument

Thomism

Henry David Thoreau

thought experiment

Thrasymachus

Paul Tillich

Topics

Tractatus Logico-Philosophicus

transcendental argument

transcendentalism

transcendental unity of
apperception

A Treatise of Human Nature

Truth and Method

truth-function

truth table

Tusculan Disputations

tychism

types, theory of

type-token distinction

Übermensch

Miguel de Unamuno

uniformity of nature

unity of science movement

universal instantiation

use-mention distinction

utilitarianism

value theory

Venn diagram

verifiability principle

Giambattista Vico

Vienna Circle

virtue ethics

vitalism

warranted assertability

The Wealth of Nations

well-formed formula

Weltaunschauung

A. N. Whitehead

will to power

Ludwig Wittgenstein

Christian Wolff

Word and Object

Xenophon

Young Hegelians

Zeno of Citium

Zeno of Elea

Zeno's paradoxes

NOTES

Introduction: On the Historical Study of Philosophy

1. G. W. F. Hegel, *Phenomenology of Spirit,* trans. A. V. Miller (New York: Oxford University Press, 1977), par. 68.

2. Quoted in Stillman Drake, *Discoveries and Opinions of Galileo* (New York: Doubleday, 1957), 224–25.

3. Quoted by Ernst Cassirer, "The Concept of Philosophy as a Philosophical Problem," in *Symbol, Myth, and Culture: Essays and Lectures of Ernst Cassirer 1935–1945,* ed. Donald Phillip Verene (New Haven: Yale University Press, 1979), 50–51.

4. Immanuel Kant, *Critique of Pure Reason,* trans. Norman Kemp Smith (London: Macmillan, 1958), A5; B9.

5. Hegel, *Phenomenology of Spirit,* par. 67.

6. Barbara Sproul, *Primal Myths: Creation Myths Around the World* (San Francisco: Harper, 1979).

7. Ernst Cassirer, *The Philosophy of Symbolic Forms,* vol. 4, *The Metaphysics of Symbolic Forms,* ed. John Michael Krois and Donald Phillip Verene, trans. John Michael Krois (New Haven: Yale University Press, 1996), 187.

8. F. E. Peters, *Greek Philosophical Terms: A Historical Lexicon* (New York: New York University Press, 1967).

Chapter 4: On Reading Philosophical Books

1. Antoine Arnauld and Pierre Nicole, *La logique, ou l'art de penser: Contenant outre les règles communes, plusieurs observations nouvelles,*

175

propres à former le judgement, ed. P. Clair and F. Girbal (Paris: Presses Universitaires de France, 1965), 299.

2. Aristotle, *Rhetoric,* 1.1–2 and 2.20–23; *Prior Analytics,* 2.27; *Topics,* 1.1.

3. A. N. Whitehead, *Process and Reality: An Essay in Cosmology* (New York: Harper, 1960), 395–96.

4. Ernesto Grassi, *Rhetoric and Philosophy: The Humanist Tradition,* trans. J. M. Krois and A. Azodi (Carbondale: Southern Illinois University Press, 2001), chap. 2.

5. Michèle Le Doeuff, *The Philosophical Imaginary,* trans. Colin Gordon (Stanford: Stanford University Press, 1989), 1.

6. R. G. Collingwood, *An Essay on Philosophical Method* (Oxford: Clarendon, 1933), 214.

7. See the translation of the passage from this fragment in *Hegel's Recollection: A Study of Images in the Phenomenology of Spirit,* by Donald Phillip Verene (Albany: State University of New York Press), 25.

8. Umberto Eco, "The *Poetics* and Us," in *On Literature,* trans. Martin McLaughlin (New York: Harcourt, 2002), 250–51.

9. Giambattista Vico, "The Academies and the Relation Between Philosophy and Eloquence," trans. D. P. Verene, in Vico, *On the Study Methods of Our Time,* trans. E. Gianturco (Ithaca: Cornell University Press, 1990), 87.

10. Susanne Langer, *Philosophy in a New Key: A Study of the Symbolism of Reason, Rite, and Art* (New York: Penguin, 1942), 114.

11. René Descartes, *The Philosophical Writings of Descartes,* vol. 2, trans. J. Cottingham, R. Stoothoff, and D. Murdoch (New York: Cambridge University Press, 1984), 16.

12. Plutarch, *Marcellus,* 14.7–9. Trzetzes, *Book of Histories,* 2.103–44, reports this as a *charistion,* a triple-pulley device. See *Greek Mathematics,* trans. Ivor Thomas, vol. 2 (Cambridge: Loeb Classical Library, Harvard University Press, 2000), 21.

13. Descartes, *Philosophical Writings,* 2:3.

14. Thomas Hobbes, *Leviathan,* ed. C. B. MacPherson (New York: Penguin, 1985), 227.

15. Ibid., chap. 44.

16. Kant, *Critique of Pure Reason*, A235–36; B294–95.

17. Ibid., A141; B180.

18. Hegel, *Phenomenology of Spirit*, par. 78.

19. Giambattista Vico, *The New Science of Giambattista Vico*, trans. T. G. Bergin and M. H. Fisch (Ithaca: Cornell University Press, 1968), par. 208.

20. Collingwood, *Essay on Philosophical Method*, 202.

21. See the translation of Brecht's remarks in Verene, *Hegel's Recollection*, 119–20.

22. Ezra Pound, *How to Read* (London: Harmsworth, 1931), 13.

23. Vico, *Study Methods*, 80.

24. See the conception of reading in Giambattista Vico, *Autobiography*, trans. Max Harold Fisch and Thomas Goddard Bergin (Ithaca: Cornell University Press, 1990), 120.

25. A. N. Whitehead, *The Aims of Education and Other Essays* (New York: Macmillan, 1929), 12.

Chapter 5: The Origin of Philosophy and the Theater of the World

1. H. B. Gottschalk, *Heraclides of Pontus* (Oxford: Clarendon, 1980).

2. C. Kerényi, *Asklepios: Archetypal Image of the Physician's Existence*, trans. R. Manheim (New York: Pantheon, 1959), 58–59. I find Kerényi's interpretation persuasive. Aristophanes gives a comedic portrait of treatment in an asclepieion, or temple of healing (*Plutus*, 653–747). The standard reference work is *Asclepius: A Collection and Interpretation of the Testimonies*, 2 vols., ed. E. S. Edelstein and L. Edelstein (Baltimore: Johns Hopkins University Press, 1945).

3. Aristotle, *The Complete Works of Aristotle*, 2 vols., ed. J. Barnes (Princeton: Princeton University Press, 1984), 2:2406.

4. Desiderius Erasmus, *The Praise of Folly*, trans. H. H. Hudson (Princeton: Princeton University Press, 1941), 10. The term "foolosophers" was coined by Sir Thomas Chaloner in the first English translation of Erasmus's work (1549).

5. René Descartes, *Cogitationes privatae*, in *Oeuvres de Descartes*, ed. C. Adam and P. Tannery, 12 vols. with suppl. (Paris: Cerf, 1897–1910), 10:213. My translation.

6. Descartes, *Les passions de l'âme*, in *Ouevres de Descartes*, 11:380. My translation.

7. Indispensable for understanding the "theater of the world" is Richard Bernheimer, "*Theatrum Mundi*," *Art Bulletin* 28 (1956): 225–47.

8. F. A. Yates, *Theatre of the World* (Chicago: University of Chicago Press, 1969).

9. Ibid., chap. 9.

10. Anthony Ashley Cooper, Third Earl of Shaftesbury, *Second Characters, or The Language of Forms*, ed. B. Rand (Cambridge: Cambridge University Press, 1914); and *The Life, Unpublished Letters and Philosophical Regimen of Anthony, Earl of Shaftesbury*, ed. B. Rand (London: Swann Sonnenschein; New York: Macmillan, 1900), 468–69, 472–74.

11. Giulio Camillo, *L'idea del theatro dell'eccellen. M. Giulio Camillo* (Florence: Lorenzo Torrentino, 1550). The copy I have used is in the National Library in Florence. On Camillo's theater, see Lina Bolzoni, *Il teatro della memoria: Studi su Giulio Camillo* (Padua: Livina, 1984); and F. A. Yates, *The Art of Memory* (Chicago: University of Chicago Press, 1966), chaps. 6–7. See also "Philosophical Memory," chap. 4 of *Philosophy and the Return to Self-Knowledge*, by D. P. Verene (New Haven: Yale University Press, 1997).

12. Marsilio Ficino, *The Letters of Marsilio Ficino*, trans. by members of the Language Department of the School of Economic Science, London (London: Shepheard-Walwyn, 1975), 1:188–90 (Letter 123).

13. Ibid., 4:30–31 (Letter 22).

14. Ibid., 3:18–21, 28–31 (Letters 13 and 18).

15. Vico, *Study Methods*, 77.

16. Giambattista Vico, *On Humanistic Education: Six Inaugural Orations 1699–1707*, trans. G. A. Pinton and A. W. Shippee (Ithaca: Cornell University Press, 1993), 138.

17. Vico, *Study Methods*, 48. See *The Digest of Justinian* (Latin text), ed. T. Mommsen and P. Krueger, English trans. and ed. A. Watson

(Philadelphia: University of Pennsylvania Press, 1985), vol. 1, book. 1, sec. 1.1.

18. Immanuel Kant, *Groundwork of the Metaphysic of Morals,* trans. H. J. Paton (New York: Harper, 1964), 83 and note.

19. Francesco Guicciardini, *Ricordi* (Milan: Rizzoli, 1977), 131. My translation.

20. Francis Bacon, *Essays Civil and Moral,* Essay 58, "Of Vicissitude of Things." Quoted by Jorge Luis Borges in "The Immortal," in *Labyrinths,* ed. D. A. Yates and J. E. Irby (New York: New Directions, 1962), 105.

21. Giovanni Pico della Mirandola, "Oration on the Dignity of Man," in *The Renaissance Philosophy of Man,* ed. E. Cassirer, P. O. Kristeller, and J. H. Randall Jr. (Chicago: University of Chicago Press, 1948), 223; *De hominis dignitate,* ed. E. Garin (Florence: Vallecchi, 1942).

22. Pico, "Oration," 226. The hermetic tradition continues into Hegel; see Glenn Alexander Magee, *Hegel and the Hermetic Tradition* (Ithaca: Cornell University Press, 2001).

23. Pico, "Oration," 235. The various meanings of Pico's principle, "Thou art," εἴ, is discussed in Plutarch's essay on "The E at Delphi" (*Moralia,* 384d–394c). See also Ernesto Grassi and Maristella Lorch, *Folly and Insanity in Renaissance Literature* (Binghamton: Center for Medieval and Early Renaissance Studies, 1986), 17–21, on the importance of the E at Delphi for the connection between rhetoric and philosophy.

24. Juan Luis Vives, "A Fable About Man," in *Renaissance Philosophy of Man,* 387; *Fabula de homine,* in Vives, *Opera omnia,* vol. 4 (London: Gregg, 1964; facsimile reprinting of the 1745 Benedicti Monfort edition).

25. Vives, "Fable About Man," 387. Compare Cicero, *De legibus,* 1.8–9; and *De natura deorum,* 2.56 and 60–61.

26. Vives, "Fable About Man," 388.

27. Camillo, *L'idea del theatro,* 7. My translation. Compare Matthew 11:15; Mark 4:23; and Luke 8.8.

28. Francis Bacon, *Novum Organon,* book 1, aphorisms 44 and 61–67.

29. Vico, *New Science,* par. 342.

30. Hegel, *Phenomenology of Spirit,* par. 5.

31. Ibid., par. 30. Hegel's presentation of the "I" is based on Ludwig Tieck's play, *Die verkehrte Welt*. See Verene, *Hegel's Recollection*, chap. 4.

32. Hegel, *Phenomenology of Spirit*, par. 801.

33. Ibid., par. 808.

34. Ibid.

35. G. W. F. Hegel, "The 'Earliest System-Programme of German Idealism' (Berne, 1796)," in *Hegel's Development: Toward the Sunlight 1770–1801*, by H. S. Harris (Oxford: Oxford University Press, 1972), 510–12.

36. Hegel, *Phenomenology of Spirit*, pars. 61–65.

37. Hegel, "System-Programme," 511.

38. Quoted by Ernst Cassirer, *Rousseau, Kant and Goethe*, trans. J. Gutmann, P. O. Kristeller, and J. H. Randall (New York: Harper, 1963), 2.

39. G. W. F. Hegel, *Grundlinien der Philosophie des Rechts*, vol. 7 of *Werke* (Frankfurt am Main: Suhrkamp, 1970), 28. My translation.

40. G. W. F. Hegel, *Natural Law*, trans. T. M. Knox (Philadelphia: University of Pennsylvania Press, 1975).

41. Ernst Cassirer, *The Myth of the State* (New Haven: Yale University Press, 1946), 262.

42. Ibid., 263.

43. See Vico's comment on Bacon's *Cogitata et visa* in *New Science*, par. 163.

44. G. W. F. Hegel, "Über Mythologie, Volksgeist und Kunst" (ms. fragment), trans. in Verene, *Hegel's Recollection*, 36–37.

45. Ernst Cassirer, "The Concept of Philosophy as a Philosophical Problem," in *Symbol, Myth, and Culture*, 60.

Chapter 6: Two Views of History and the History of Philosophy

1. Giambattista Vico, *The First New Science*, trans. Leon Pompa (Cambridge: Cambridge University Press, 2002) and *New Science*, trans. Bergin and Fisch.

2. G. W. F. Hegel, *Introduction to the Philosophy of History*, trans. L. Rauch (Indianapolis: Hackett, 1988); *Lectures on the Philosophy of History*, trans. J. Sibree (London, 1858); *Lectures on the History of Philosophy*, 3 vols., trans. E. S. Haldane and F. H. Simson (Atlantic Highlands: Humanities, 1983).

3. Ernst Cassirer, *An Essay on Man: An Introduction to a Philosophy of Culture* (New Haven: Yale University Press, 1944), 178.

4. A classic mid-twentieth-century example of the philosophy of history in this methodological manner, and still of interest today, is William Dray, *Laws and Explanation in History* (Oxford: Oxford University Press, 1957).

5. Hegel, "System-Programme," 510–12.

6. Giambattista Vico, *On the Most Ancient Wisdom of the Italians Unearthed from the Origins of the Latin Language*, trans. L. M. Palmer (Ithaca: Cornell University Press, 1988), 77.

7. Karl-Otto Apel, *Die Idee der Sprache in der Tradition des Humanismus von Dante bis Vico*, 2nd ed. (Bonn: Bouvier Verlag Herbert Grundmann, 1975), 320–21.

8. Ernesto Grassi, *Macht des Bildes: Ohnmacht der rationalen Sprache: Zur Reitung des Rhetorischen* (Cologne: M. DuMont Schauberg, 1970), 194.

9. These connections run throughout Grassi's work, but of particular interest may be *Rhetoric as Philosophy: The Humanist Tradition* (University Park: Pennsylvania State University Press, 1980) and *Vico and Humanism: Essays on Vico, Heidegger, and Rhetoric* (New York: Peter Lang, 1990).

10. Eugenio Garin, *L'umanesimo italiano* (1952; Bari: Laterza, 1984), 100, 110, 253. Garin sees Vico as a true thinker of the eighteenth century and not simply as the summation of the Renaissance. See his essay "Vico and the Heritage of Renaissance Thought," in *Vico: Past and Present*, ed. Giorgio Tagliacozzo (Atlantic Highlands: Humanities, 1981), pt. 1, 99–116.

11. Eugenio Garin, *Lo zodiaco della vita* (Bari: Laterza, 1976), chap. 1.

12. Donald R. Kelley, "The Theory of History," in *The Cambridge History of Renaissance Philosophy*, ed. Charles B. Schmitt and Quentin Skinner (Cambridge: Cambridge University Press, 1988), 746–61.

13. Isaiah Berlin, *Vico and Herder: Two Studies in the History of Ideas* (New York: Viking, 1976).

14. Ernst Cassirer, *The Individual and the Cosmos in Renaissance Philosophy,* trans. Mario Domandi (New York: Harper, 1963), 1. In *The Myth of the State,* Cassirer regards Hegel's "owl of Minerva" conception of philosophy as one of the most problematic features of his thought.

15. Ernst Cassirer, *The Logic of the Cultural Sciences: Five Studies,* trans. S. G. Lofts (New Haven: Yale University Press, 2000), Study 3.

16. Ernst Cassirer, *The Philosophy of the Enlightenment,* trans. F. C. A. Koelln and J. P. Pettegrove (Boston: Beacon, 1955), vi.

17. Hegel, *Grundlinien der Philosophie des Rechts,* 28. My translation.

18. James Joyce, *Finnegans Wake* (London: Faber and Faber, 1939), 452.

19. Vico, *New Science,* par. 349.

20. Paul Oskar Kristeller, *Renaissance Thought and the Arts* (Princeton: Princeton University Press, 1990), 27.

21. Vico, *New Science,* pars. 786 and 817.

22. Ibid., par. 1106.

23. Elio Gianturco, introduction to Vico, *Study Methods,* xxi.

24. Kristeller, *Renaissance Thought,* 244.

25. On imaginative universals, see Donald Phillip Verene, *Vico's Science of Imagination* (Ithaca: Cornell University Press, 1981), chap. 3.

26. See my translation, "The Academies and the Relation Between Philosophy and Eloquence," in Vico, *Study Methods,* 87.

27. As quoted in Donald R. Kelley, *Renaissance Humanism* (Boston: Twayne, 1991), 75.

28. Andrea Battistini, "Vico and Rhetoric," *New Vico Studies* 12 (1994): 8–9.

INDEX

The lists and outline have not been indexed.

Abdala the Saracen, 118
Academy of Oziosi, 143
Actaeon, 46
Aeneas, 97
Aeschines, 100
Agamemnon, 114
Alberti, Leon Battisti, 115
Anchises, 97
Anglo-American analytic
    philosophy, 14–15, 85
Anselm of Canterbury, Saint, 86
Apel, Karl-Otto, 130
Apollo, 111
Aquinas. *See* Thomas Aquinas, Saint
Archimedes, 92–93
Aristo of Chios, 114
Aristophanes, 110–11
Aristotle, 25, 80, 86, 131, 134, 138,
    139; on circular motion, 141–42;
    on imitation, 119; on Pythagoras,
    112; and Renaissance philosophy,
    45–46; on rhetoric, 152; and
    tetralogy, 10–12; on topics and
    metaphor, 90–91; on wonder,
    114
Arnauld, Antoine, 79–80
ars critica, 79–83, 99, 150
ars topica, 79–83, 99, 150
Asclepius, 110–11
Atlas, 106

Augustine of Hippo, Saint, 86, 121,
    124
Austin, J. L., 153, 158

Bacon, Francis, 53, 86, 132;
    "Idol of the Theater," 121; on
    investigation of nature, 94; on
    novelty, 118; principle of "think
    and see," 124
Battistini, Andrea, 143
Beatrice, 143
Bellona, 143
Bembo, Bernardo, 116
Bergson, Henri, 153
Berkeley, George, 54, 87
Blanshard, Brand, 153
Boccaccio, Giovanni, 116
Boehme, Jacob, 132
Borges, Jorge Luis, 118
Brandt, Sebastian, 116
Brecht, Bertold, 102
Bréhier, Emil, 86
Brucker, Jacob, 131
Bruni, Leonardo, 46
Bruno, Giordano, 115, 131, 133
Burckhardt, Jacob, 132

Cambridge Platonism, 158
Camillo, Giulio, 115–16, 118,
    120–21

Campanella, Tommaso, 130, 131
canon, the, xi–xiv, 10, 12–15
Cardano, Girolamo, 131
Cassirer, Ernst, 16, 46, 124–25, 128, 132–35
Castiglione, Baldesar, 116
Cavalcanti, Giovanni, 116
Cebes, 109–10
Cepheus, 106
Christ, 120
Cicero, 115, 131, 134, 140–41; definition of wisdom, 112; on irony and eloquence, 80, 100, 103, 104; on origin of philosophy, 106–7; on rhetoric, 87–89; on Socrates, 91, 112; triad of *sapientia, eloquentia,* and *prudentia,* 117
Collingwood, R. G., 87, 101, 153
critical realists, 15
critical thinking, 7–8
Crito, 110–11

Dante, 97–98, 138
David, 119
Demosthenes, 88
Derrida, Jacques, 14–15
Descartes, René, 53–54, 86, 92–93, 98, 103, 144, 150; his method, 81, 140–41; and *theatrum mundi,* 113–14, 120; use of Archimedes, 92–93
Dewey, John, 10
Diogenes, Laertius, 107
Dionysus I and II, 109

Eco, Umberto, 15, 88
eloquence, 88–89, 104, 117, 140
Empedocles, 105, 108
Epictetus, 114

Epicureanism, 131, 137, 138
Erasmus, Desiderius, 113, 116
Euclid, 54
existentialism, 15, 65

Fichte, Johann Gottlieb, 123, 134
Ficino, Marsilio, 116–17, 130, 131, 132, 134
Fludd, Robert, 115
foolosophers, 113
Foucault, Michel, 14–15

Gadamer, Hans-Georg, 14–15
Galileo, 9, 54
Garin, Eugenio, 130
Genesis, book of, 25
Gianturco, Elio, 140
Goethe, Johann Wolfgang von, 10
Goodman, Nelson, 14–15
Grassi, Ernesto, 83–84, 130
Greek Academy, 88, 105–6, 131
Guazzo, Stefano, 116
Guicciardini, Francesco, 118

Habermas, Jürgen, 14–15
Hadot, Pierre, 25
Hegel, G. W. F., 54, 86, 87, 97–99; metaphor of the journey, 97–98; on nature of philosophy, 5, 45; philosophy of history, 127–44; on poetry, 87; sense of humor, 102; and tetralogy, 10–12; and "theater of history," 121–24
Heidegger, Martin, 87, 135
Heraclides of Pontus, 105–8
Heraclitus, 86
Herder, Johann Gottfried von, 130
Herodotus, 82, 129, 130
Hesiod, 111
Hiero of Syracuse, 92

Hippocrates, 82
Hirsch, E. D., Jr., 157–58
Hobbes, Thomas, 94–96, 98
Homer, 138
Horace, 87, 118, 148
Hume, David, 54, 87, 134
Husserl, Edmund, 87
Huygens, Christian, 54

Iamblichus, 107
ingenium, 99
irony, 99–102

James, William, 153, 157
Job, book of, 94
Joyce, James, 124, 136
Juno, 119
Jupiter, 119–20, 124

Kant, Immanuel, 54, 87, 96–97, 98,
     134; conception of providence,
     137; conception of prudence,
     118; island metaphor, 96; and
     tetralogy, 10–12
Kepler, Johannes, 54
Kristeller, Paul Oskar, 138, 140

Landino, Cristoforo, 130
Langer, Susanne, 15, 91
Lavinia, 97
Le Doeuff, Michèle, 86
Leibniz, Georg Wilhelm, 10, 54,
     86, 134
Leon, Tyrant of Phlius, 106–8
Leonardo da Vinci, 132
Lessing, Gotthold Ephraim, 37
Levi, Albert William, 54, 65
Leviathan, 94
Levinas, Emmanuel, 14–15
liberal arts, 5, 8

Locke, John, 10, 54, 87
logical empiricism, 65
logical positivism, 15
logopoioi, 129
Lyceum, 106
Lycurgus, 106
Lyotard, Jean-François, 15

Machiavelli, Niccolò, 86, 132
MacIntyre, Alasdair, 15
Marcellus, 92
Marcus Aurelius, 114
Marx, Karl, 10, 87
Medici, 117
memory, 123, 139; as mother of
     Muses, 124; and philosophy,
     5–6, 8, 104, 144; theater of, 101,
     115–16
metaphor, 99; and argument, 84,
     87–88; Aristotle on, 90; and
     Descartes, 93; and Hegel, 98;
     and irony, 99–101; and Kant, 97;
     Langer on, 91–92
Mill, John Stuart, 87
Mohammed, 118
Muses, 124, 137
Myth of Er, 110, 122

Neo-Platonists, 114, 120
Nestor, 106
New Realists, 15
Newton, Isaac, 54
Nicholas of Cusa, 53, 133
Nicole, Pierre, 79–80

Ockham. *See* William of Ockham
Odysseus, 97, 143
Ovid, 141
Owl of Minerva, 123–24, 130,
     135–36, 143

Pascal, Blaise, 87
Peirce, C. S., 157
Peters, F. E., 16
Petrarch, Francesco, 45, 130
Phaedo, 109
philia, 107, 157
Philolaus, 109
philology, 7, 83
philosopher's dilemma, 113
Pico della Mirandola, Giovanni, 116, 131, 134; and community of philosophers, 120–21; connected to Vico, 130; his oration on dignity of man, 118–19
Plato, 25, 53, 86, 99, 105, 134, 138, 139; conception of philosophy, 102, 120; dialogues, 99; doctrine of form, 82; and memory, 118, 122–23; and tetralogy, 10–12; view of poetry, 93
Platonic Academy. *See* Greek Academy
Pliny, 12
Plotinus, 114, 116
Plutarch, 92
Poliziano, Angelo, 130
Pomponazzi, Pietro, 134
Port-Royal Logic (Arnauld and Nicole), 79–81
Pound, Ezra, 103
pragmatism, 157
Prester John, 96
Prometheus, 106
Pythagoras, 105–9, 112, 120, 123, 157

Quine, W. V. O., 14–15, 87
Quintilian, 89, 117, 147–48

Ramus, Peter, 131
Rawls, John, 14–15
rhetoric, 87–89, 96; and argument, 6, 83–84, 152; as feature of philosophical books, 81
Robinson Crusoe, 96
Roman law, 118
Rousseau, Jean-Jacques, 141
Russell, Bertrand, 87, 153

sacred texts, 12–13
Salutati, Collucio, 130
Schweitzer, Albert, 125
Scylax, 129
self-knowledge, 101, 119, 122, 138
Sellars, Wilfred, 14–15
Shaftesbury, Anthony Ashley Cooper, Third Earl of, 115, 158
Shakespeare, William, 115, 143
Sigonio, Carlo, 143
Simmias, 109–10
skepticism, 138
Smith, Adam, 87
Socrates, 114, 139, 150; conception of philosophy, 6, 91, 101, 108–12, 120; pursuit of self-knowledge, 138; sense of humor, 102; use of question and metaphor, 99–100
Solomon, 118
sōphrosynē, 113
speculative thinking, 7–8, 123, 125
Spinoza, Benedict, 86, 124
Sproul, Barbara, 12
Stoicism, 138; paired with Epicureanism, 131, 137; and theater of the world, 114–16
Strawson, P. F., 14–15
Strepsiades, 111

syllogism, 80–81, 90
theatrum mundi, 113, 121
Thersites, 114
Thomas Aquinas, Saint, 134
Thucydides, 130

Ulysses, 106

Valla, Lorenzo, 130
Vanini, Giulio Cesare, 131
Vico, Giambattista, 83, 88, 121,
    124; on eloquence, 117; on irony,
    100; philosophy of history, 127–
    44; on topics, 90; on wisdom, 103

Vignaux, Paul, 38
Virgil, 143
Vitruvius, 115
Vives, Juan Luis, 116, 119, 124, 130

Whitehead, A. N., 54, 82, 104, 153
Wilde, Oscar, 102
William of Ockham, 86
Wittgenstein, Ludwig, 87, 158

Xanthus, 129
Xenophon, 100

Zeus, 14, 110